New Modes

Redefining Practice

ARCHITECTURAL
DESIGN

September/October 2018
Profile No 255

ISSN 0003-8504
ISBN 978 1119 328148

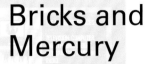

Editorial Offices
John Wiley & Sons
9600 Garsington Road
Oxford
OX4 2DQ

T +44 (0)1865 776868

Consultant Editor
Helen Castle

Managing Editor
Caroline Ellerby
Caroline Ellerby Publishing

Freelance Contributing Editor
Abigail Grater

Publisher
Paul Sayer

Art Direction + Design
CHK Design:
Christian Küsters

Production Editor
Elizabeth Gongde

Prepress
Artmedia, London

Printed in Italy by Printer
Trento Srl

Journal Customer Services
For ordering information,
claims and any enquiry
concerning your journal
subscription please go to
www.wileycustomerhelp
.com/ask or contact your
nearest office.

Americas
E: cs-journals@wiley.com
T: +1 781 388 8598 or
+1 800 835 6770 (toll free
in the USA & Canada)

**Europe, Middle East
and Africa**
E: cs-journals@wiley.com
T: +44 (0)1865 778315

Asia Pacific
E: cs-journals@wiley.com
T: +65 6511 8000

Japan (for Japanese-
speaking support)
E: cs-japan@wiley.com
T: +65 6511 8010 or 005 316
50 480 (toll-free)

Visit our Online Customer
Help available in 7 languages
at www.wileycustomerhelp
.com/ask

Print ISSN: 0003-8504
Online ISSN: 1554-2769

Prices are for six issues
and include postage and
handling charges. Individual-
rate subscriptions must be
paid by personal cheque or
credit card. Individual-rate
subscriptions may not be
resold or used as library
copies.

All prices are subject to
change without notice.

Identification Statement
Periodicals Postage paid
at Rahway, NJ 07065.
Air freight and mailing in
the USA by Mercury Media
Processing, 1850 Elizabeth
Avenue, Suite C, Rahway,
NJ 07065, USA.

USA Postmaster
Please send address changes
to *Architectural Design*,
John Wiley & Sons Inc.,
c/o The Sheridan Press,
PO Box 465, Hanover,
PA 17331, USA

Rights and Permissions
Requests to the Publisher
should be addressed to:
Permissions Department
John Wiley & Sons Ltd
The Atrium
Southern Gate
Chichester
West Sussex PO19 8SQ
UK

F: +44 (0)1243 770 620
E: Permissions@wiley.com

Subscribe to ⚠
⚠ is published bimonthly
and is available to purchase
on both a subscription basis
and as individual volumes
at the following prices.

Prices
Individual copies:
£29.99 / US$45.00
Individual issues on
⚠ App for iPad:
£9.99 / US$13.99
Mailing fees for print
may apply

Annual Subscription Rates
Student: £90 / US$137
print only
Personal: £136 / US$215
print and iPad access
Institutional: £310 / US$580
print or online
Institutional: £388 / US$725
combined print and online
6-issue subscription on
⚠ App for iPad: £44.99 /
US$64.99

Front cover: Graphic
design by Christian
Küsters/CHK Design. ©
John Wiley & Sons Ltd.

Inside front cover:
raumlaborberlin,
Initiative Haus der
Statistik, Berlin Mitte,
2015. © raumlaborberlin

Page 1: 00, Diagram
of the distributed
manufacturing network of
WikiHouse, 2015. © 00

⚠ ARCHITECTURAL DESIGN

September/October
2018

Profile No.
255

05/2018

MIX
Paper from
responsible sources
FSC® C015829
www.fsc.org

alma-nac's Chris Bryant,
Tristan Wigfall
and Caspar Rodgers

Chris Bryant, Caspar Rodgers and Tristan Wigfall met while studying for their Architecture Diplomas at the Bartlett School of Architecture, University College London (UCL) in 2006. They founded alma-nac in 2010 after a period of working for larger practices in London and San Francisco.

Alma-nac began on a market stall with their first project, Free Architecture (2010), a method of engaging with the general public, offering advice and consultations to anyone who passed by their pitches on Portabello Road and London's Southbank. Beginning with the idea that good design should be available to all, start with a conversation and be clear and accessible, they used the stall to promote their belief that architecture does not need to be resource intensive or excessively polished, and is more than a shiny object. These core principles continue to resonate throughout their work.

The practice has since developed a strong 'research through action' methodology, embracing values of craft and craftiness, which is evident in their early work delivered in testing environments. Examples included the Incredible Edible Gingerbread House (Brunswick Centre, London, 2011), in which a million calories were devoured in three days by 2,000 children; Balls! (Arup Headquarters, London, 2014), an open-source interactive kinetic installation in collaboration with Ruairi Glynn; and the Slim House (London, 2011), a 2.3-metre (7.5-foot) wide three-bedroom family house. This early experimental work led to larger projects including co-housing schemes inspired by the Slim House; low-cost workspaces in high-cost areas; and an innovative animal hospital focused on relaxing pet owners. In July 2015 alma-nac was named one of the 'emerging architectural talents' of the world by *Wallpaper** magazine as part of its Architects' Directory, and in 2016 was one of three winners in the Royal Academy of Arts' 'Urban Jigsaw' ideas competition looking at new and innovative approaches to address brownfield sites in the capital.

Always about more than the projects delivered by the team, alma-nac recognise the importance and benefit of being part of a wider community, and how the furthering of the profession of architecture is advantageous to all. They seek to expand the notion of architectural practice and make the process transparent and accessible. In 2010 they set up the Emerging Group, a place for young architects to meet, share ideas and collaborate, as a direct response to the recession and the low morale within the profession. Since then they have held a variety of positions at a number of architecture institutions: Chris Bryant was chair of the Royal Institute of British Architects (RIBA) Small Practice Group and Guerrilla Tactics Conference Steering Group, has taught at Birmingham Institute of Art and Design, and currently teaches at the University of Westminster, London. Caspar Rodgers is a member of the RIBA Client Liaison Group and has taught at Oxford Brookes University. Tristan Wigfall has led educational workshops at the Architecture Foundation and is part of the London School of Architecture Practice Network.

Every alma-nac project is a collective effort. Other members of the core team, past and present, include Alice Aldrin-Schrepfer, Simon Campbell, Adam Currie, Victoria Dean, Marta Kruger, Joe Reilly, Adam Shapland and Kieran Wardle. Beyond this, alma-nac has been fortunate to work with many other inspiring organisations and individuals. It is the richness and diversity of these collaborations that drives the practice forward. ⅅ

The Changing Forms and Values of Architectural Practice

Forensic Architecture,
Rafah: Black Friday,
1–4 August 2014

Working in the crossover between architecture,
politics and law, Forensic Architecture draw
on input from a wide range of collaborators to
create spatial evidence rather than buildings.
This 'Image-Complex' illustrates how 3D
models provide an optical device and a means
of composing the relation between multiple
images and videos in space and time.

INTRODUCTION

CHRIS BRYANT, CASPAR RODGERS
AND TRISTAN WIGFALL OF ALMA-NAC

Architecture appears as the exercise of an arcane and privileged aesthetic code.

—Reyner Banham, 'A Black Box: The Secret Profession of Architecture', 1990[1]

The architectural profession has siloed itself. With increasing focus placed on image and form, the agency of the professional architect can be seen to have steadily diminished over the last 50 years. As the environments in which architects work grow in complexity, official reports chart the demise of the profession.[2] Routes to building no longer necessarily start with the architect; what remains of the architect's services, reduced to accommodate other statutory, construction and management specialists, now occupies a smaller space in the decision-making process. However, there is a growing practice of architecture that is breaking free from this mould, embracing the complexities of politics and people and finally admitting that architecture without these influences is just glorified furniture design. This new mode of practice is emerging with a very different set of role models, creating new types of outputs that relate to a very different set of values. While the profession begins to wither, the discipline of architecture is re-emerging.

But are these new values being expressed in the form of architectural practice? If so, what are the 'new modes of practice' that are emerging, and are they actually new at all, or merely recycled structures and ideologies played out in a new field?

New Modes Versus Old Modes

The role of architects can cover a huge range of activities and values, altering according to the project, and the subsequent mode of practice they employ follows suit. The role is notoriously hard to adequately define without the definition becoming overly limiting. However, in order to distinguish what we mean by a 'new mode' of architectural practice, it is necessary to establish what we understand to be the traditional form. Russian-American novelist Ayn Rand's Howard Roarke, the fictional lead character of her book *The Fountainhead*, written in 1943,[3] would sadly have us believe the architect is the sole tortured ego sitting between the property mogul and the ultimate purity of spatial expression.

A little less impassioned, in 1997 Renzo Piano stated: 'Architects are people who know … why and how houses, bridges, and cities are built'.[4] The subsections of the 'how' and 'why' have been in varying degrees of flux since the role of the architect separated from that of the master builder around 1600,[5] and the profession was born. Rate of change has been particularly rapid over the last 70 years, the 'how' of building becoming vastly complex, and the 'why' reacting to the growing influence of the private sector. As set out in Finn Williams's article (see pp 104–9), architects have shifted away from the state-employed practice typical of the 1950s

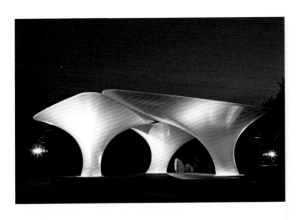

Zaha Hadid,
Pavilion/Aqua Table,
2005

When a Zaha table looks just look a Zaha building, then you know you are in some kind of trouble – a visual comparison made by Jeremy Till in his 'Beyond the Fountainhead' lecture, indicating how some of the current values of contemporary architecture are so close to pure shape making as to be indistinguishable from that of furniture design.

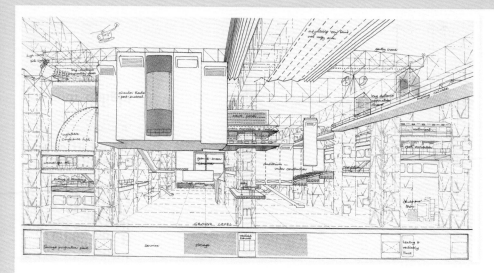

to the 1970s towards the private sector, with the proportion of
architects practising in the public sector dropping from 49 per
cent in 1976 to 0.7 per cent in 2017. It is this fairly recent arrival
at a profession dominated by private practice that forms the
status quo for this issue of Δ.

Architectural output is set by the agenda of architect, client
and regulatory bodies combined. Working within the state,
the focus of this output was often on longer-term value to
the community. With the pronounced global shift towards
neoliberalism since the 1980s,[6] however, this agenda is now
more financially driven and often shorter-term in outlook.
Within the building industry, the subsequent introduction of
early design role specialisms, such as planning consultants
and project managers, alongside changes in typical
procurement routes, such as the contractor-led approach,
have all impacted the architect's services. As a profession,
architecture has seen its influence wane; the architect
becoming one of a myriad of specialist consultants whose
contribution to a project is all but pre-decided. In the tightly
worded appointment documents relating to the delivery of
highly complex constructions, there is no space left for the
indefinite role. Outputs must be pre-established in black and
white, and focused on risk management and financial goals.
Roles are specialised and compartmentalised and that of the
architect has been edited down accordingly.

With this curtailment of the role has come a loss of agency,
further cemented through the self-siloing of the discipline, and
reinforced through the profession's reading of its own history
as both purely formal and, critically, almost entirely distinct
from that of its wider environment,[7] 'privileging the building
over its occupation … over the processes of production … and
over the way it situates itself in society'.[8] This objectification
of the output of the discipline is encouraged through the
methods of teaching at key influential schools of architecture.[9]
Teaching and practising architecture relative to the history
of architecture, a self-referential story of form, occasionally
function, hardly ever of socioeconomic context or actual end-
use, posits that the true value of a building is too idiosyncratic
for all to understand, and must ultimately be taken on trust.
Not the best starting point for the commercial justification of
the architect's role.

In the midst of all this, however, in 2015 a young studio
collective called Assemble, sitting clearly apart from this
current mode of practice, won the Turner Prize, the most

Neave Brown/London Borough of Camden Architects Department,
Alexandra Road Estate (Rowley Way),
Camden,
London,
1979

Designed in 1968 by Neave Brown, the scheme included 520 homes alongside a school, community centre, youth club and parks. Brown's aim was not one of maximising the site's financial potential, but of integrating the built form with open space while creating low-rise, repetitive and anonymous homes that replicated the characteristics he saw as the true virtues of traditional housing.

alma-nac,
Paxton House, Croydon,
London,
2017

Renovation and extension of an office block to accommodate 43 homes, along with co-living facilities including a spare bedroom shared by the block. The scheme forms part of the practice's ongoing research into methods of positively activating awkward sites in response to London's housing shortage.

prestigious of British contemporary art awards. Their project, Granby Four Streets (completed in 2017), was the renovation of a series of traditional terraced houses in collaboration with the local community in Liverpool (see p 16). This highlighted the existence of what can be described as a 'quiet revolution' in the architectural profession. A new breed of architect is emerging, challenging the limitations of current typical practice. As Williams puts it, returning to 'the social idealism, freedom to experiment and scale of ambition' of an earlier era, rejecting the 1980s' architecture school of built form fetishisation yet this time with a new set of tools to play with; no longer subscribing to less is more, but closer aligned with mess is the law. Alma-nac's work is part of this revolution, as one of many practices exploring this new mode of practice, the output of which need not be devoid of aesthetic control, but rather defined by values that are not purely financial. Our recently completed Paxton House scheme in London (2017) marries these two aspects in the continuation of a self-driven research project into new forms of constrained living requirements, but in a product whose value is in part still tied to its form.

Catalysts and Context

Recognising the causes of change is crucial to understanding the potential impact of this 'revolution' on the architectural profession as a whole. The catalysts are contextual. A globalised context could be argued to stem from Western capitalist trends, from the four threats to localism Brian McGrath maps out in his contribution to the issue (pp 50–57). Many will be both shared worldwide and Western-centric. However, as emerging markets grow to form the majority of global construction, with an estimated growth of 128 per cent by 2020 resulting in a 55 per cent share of global construction',[10] a far wider set of local influences is just as critical to comprehend. So are the catalysts for this change in the architectural profession global or local, born from scarcity of environment or window of opportunity? Douglas Murphy's clarification of the diminishing role of the architect (pp 14–21) is a clear enough impetus. His analysis of the profession's history of 'constitutive crises', specific to the UK,

EXYZT and Agnes Denes,
The Dalston Mill,
Hackney,
London,
2009

This temporary wheat field, functioning flour mill and bakery served to connect local communities with the new incoming populations of a rapidly changing area. EXYZT refused to accept architecture as an isolated discipline – their manifesto went so far as to state they refused to enter the current world of architectural practice, a system solely serving the building industry.

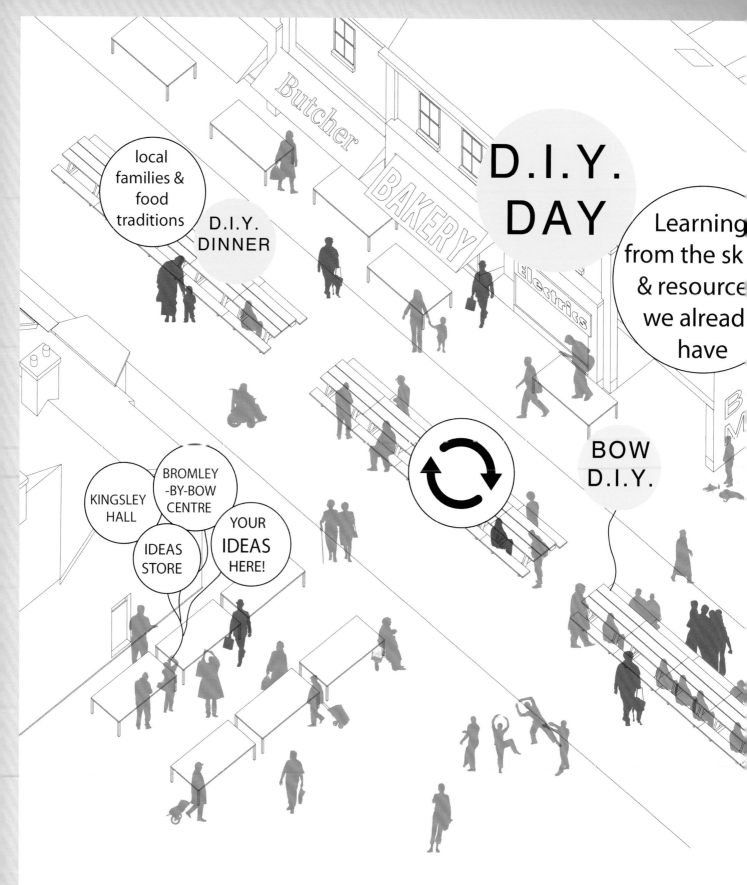

Alma-nac's Bow DIY project, undertaken in 2012 in collaboration with Architecture 00, was a similar example, a research and communication exercise setting out to map and unlock a population's skill set in a specific area of London.

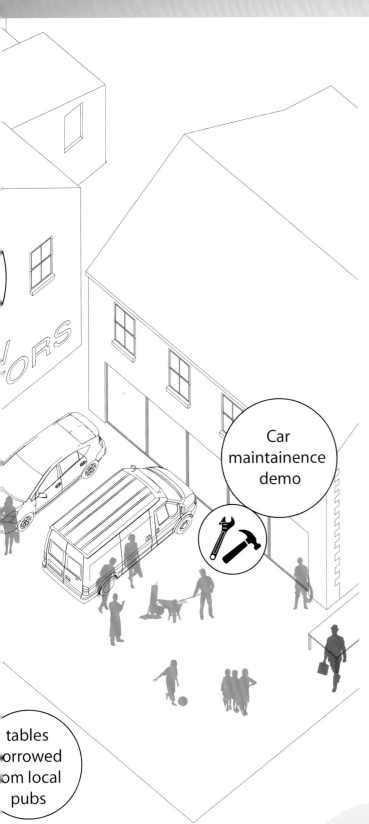

Car
maintainence
demo

tables
orrowed
om local
pubs

alma-nac and
Architecture 00,
Bow DIY,
Bow, London,
2012

In exploring the theme of
urban 'scarcity', alma-nac and
Architecture 00 set up hubs to
expose local skills, then mapped
and linked these with existing
learning infrastructures.

paints a colourful picture of the drivers of change. The causes are multitudinous, but three main patterns emerge – financial pressure versus new value; new routes to change; and the political/environmental condition – and it is around these themes that this issue of 𝔻 is organised.

Today, architects are typically paid less for their services than their professional counterparts/predecessors. At the same time, new values are emerging within the realm of architectural production, seeping slowly back into the profession. These extend beyond the finite production of buildings. Indy Johar's reframing of the value of architecture as that of social and economic over the physical illustrates one such example, positioning his practice, Architecture 00, in a very different stream of work (see Helen Castle's interview with him on pp 78–85). Alma-nac's Bow DIY project, undertaken in 2012 in collaboration with Architecture 00, was a similar example, a research and communication exercise setting out to map and unlock a population's skill set in a specific area of London. Indy's calculations show that the cost of construction makes up a fractional proportion of the financial cycle of a building, a viewpoint that has the potential to change what is deemed 'costly' in building, 'thereby driving a systemically different "architecture" judged on its performative effect. This is an architecture that moves beyond the media shot to the long-term impact and influence over human behaviour.'[11]

With this change of perspective encompassing a wider set of values come new routes to architectural production. In the case of Rotterdam-based Killing Architects (see pp 30–37) this involved a deliberate, wholesale move away from building as their form of architectural production. For others not completely divorced from the built form, there comes a shift away from polished construction as the celebrated output, and with this the potential for a reduced technical barrier to entry. These new avenues of exploration are thus available without the necessary procurement behemoth battling practice structures, sometimes without even the requirement for apprenticeships in practice. New routes to genuine architectural agency outside of the stranglehold of the current systems of spatial influence are numerous. Roles previously treated as 'other' to the traditional architect are being subsumed, for example in the practice of Carl Turner Architects (pp 44–49) where they are builder, developer, curator and, ultimately, client for their own work. Elsewhere, client types are changing top-down wealth to bottom-up connected communities, providing opportunities to return to exploration and testing, and learning through doing. The Burnside Skatepark in Portland, Oregon, officially endorsed in 1993, is a fantastic example of both such a process and resulting product, a method of urban intervention being toted as one of 'visualising citizenship',[12] its precedent causing an explosion of similarly inspired projects.

Then there are architects whose work responds to the vacuums of state, whether the physical legacy of failed state operations, or the opportunities found within slow and complex bureaucratic systems. These practices are working at the micro local level, such as studioBASAR's introduction of social spaces in Bucharest, Romania (pp 38–43) or GutGut's creation of communities within former industrial buildings in Bratislava, Slovakia (pp 98–103). They are also operating at the macro level, for example atelier d'architecture autogérée's fusion as both non-governmental organisation and interdisciplinary design studio (pp 58–65). Globalisation in and of itself presents possibilities for the exploration of new practice; Zoohaus Collective's Inteligencias Colectivas initiative (pp 66–71) operates across scale spectrums combining local skill sets with globalised construction knowledge, then seeding new vernaculars via open-source sharing of the outcomes. Simply the return to genuinely locally responsive design becomes new in the current financially focused environment; New Jersey-based Hector's efforts in this department explore the reality of socially contextual design in extremely complex and deeply rooted modern urban environments, their designs responding to 'multiple conflicting narratives' (see pp 86–91).

Four Families of New Modes
This ᐰ brings together a series of practising groups and organises them according to four predominant trends, each of which is preceded with a foundational piece to establish the context within which these specific subsets of pioneers work.

(1) Diversification of the Role:
New practice types entrepreneurial in spirit, this brings together those architects whose work steps on the toes of the disciplines around them, climbing up the food chain to take the role of project initiator or developer, or reclaiming territory lost in the wave of specialisation as their primary output, utilising their wider skill sets to offer new types of services.

(2) The Power of Localism:
A new breed of practice returning to localised action, as agents for change within existing communities developing briefs, places and organisations, facilitating community building and rearticulating region-specific design. In place, reverting to the locally embedded professional, yet modifying this position with new practice modalities.

(3) The Architect as Disruptor:
The all-out disruptors – the small family of practices whose work either sets out to destabilise the financial/political structures in which they operate, or doubles as a form of activism.

Burnside Skatepark,
Portland,
Oregon,
1993

Starting life as a series of illegally constructed concrete banks, this skatepark was designed, built, managed and funded by the local skateboarding community. Iterative negotiations with local authorities saw the scheme retrospectively approved. The park has fundamentally changed both the local area, but also the wider approach to designing and building skateparks.

alma-nac,
Co-working and community
space,
Southwark,
London,
2017-

Proposed scheme for activating a disused, local authority-owned building at the base of a housing block to provide a community workspace hub.

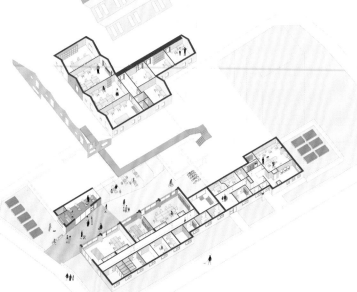

(4) Policy, Strategy and Common Good:

Working far upstream of the drawing board, these practices employ broader strategies in the creation of our towns and cities, be that influencing policy, redefining value or working outside of the realm of the building as product.

Is it Real, is it Right, is it Viable?

So are these new modes of practice indicative of a genuine change in the profession? And as professional practice rather than hobby, do they need to be financial viable to be eligible for such a characterisation? Are such changes an expansion of the role of the architect, or an escape from it? Architecture has always reinvented itself, so is this new typology just one more iteration, or something altogether different? How can we know whether it is something more than just the ongoing natural flux? Are the practices included in this issue indicative of a genuine new direction, or just a creative hernia? Shumi Bose's article (pp 22–9) is key here, asking 'Firstly, whether such an "expansion" is appropriate'. She argues that to answer this question we must first establish whether we define architectural practice as 'a service industry, a creative field or a commercial enterprise'. We can perhaps add to this assessment. Measuring architecture as a profession, this evolution must in some way be tested through its financial viability. Ignoring the capacity for payment of services comes with the ugly association of a return to the worthy hobby of the privileged. Yet in moving away from commercial agendas, as many of the practices within this issue clearly are, there is an inherent requirement to adopt a new set of values. These may well exhibit longer lag times to demonstrate their work, yet proof of their impact on society may be required before architects' fees can be justified. Whether currently paying their way or not, the architects in this Δ may yet prove to be the seeds of a new mode of architectural practice. Δ

Notes

1. Reyner Banham, 'A Black Box: The Secret Profession of Architecture', *New Statesman & Society*, 3 (122), 12 October 1990, pp 24–5.
2. Claire Jamieson, Dickon Robinson, John Worthington and Caroline Cole, *The Future for Architects*, Building Futures and RIBA, February 2010: www.buildingfutures.org.uk/projects/building-futures/the-future-for-architects.
3. Ayn Rand, *The Fountainhead*, The Bobbs-Merrill Company (New York), 1943.
4. Renzo Piano and Kenneth Frampton, 'Preface', *The Renzo Piano Logbook*, Thames & Hudson (London), 1997.
5. Arnold Pacy, *Medieval Architectural Drawing*, Tempus Publishing (Stroud), 2007, pp 225–7.
6. Jonathan D Ostry, Prakash Loungani and Davide Furceri, 'Neoliberalism: Oversold?', *Finance & Development*, 53 (2), June 2016: www.imf.org/external/pubs/ft/fandd/2016/06/ostry.htm.
7. Jeremy Till, 'Beyond the Fountainhead', lecture at the Columbia GSAPP Studio-X, Rio de Janeiro, 7 August 2014: www.youtube.com/watch?v=edpC6VgKWG4.
8. *Mies Magazine* interview with Jeremy Till, December 2013: www.youtube.com/watch?v=gHsVKv40M14.
9. Jeremy Till, *Architecture Depends*, MIT Press (Cambridge, MA), 2009, p 8.
10. Jamieson, Robinson, Worthington and Cole, *op cit*, p 1.
11. Indy Johar, 'Towards a Future Architecture: 3 Revolutions & 9 Ideas reinvent architecture & design v 13.08.15', blog post: https://medium.com/architecture-00/redesigning-architecture-7e8aeccb7dc3
12. Iain Borden, 'Skatopia', *Skateboarding and the City: A Complete History*, Bloomsbury (London), 2019, forthcoming.

what if:projects,
Livesy Exchange, London,
2018

Crossing the boundary between community enabler, architect and infrastructure designers, what if: projects guide projects with goals ranging from increasing the transparency of local planning activity through to designing and financing the regeneration of overlooked community spaces. Livesy Exchange began with the conversion of 60 garages on the Ledbury Estate on Old Kent Road into a multi-use community skills and industry space, but following fire issues on the tower, strong local support has seen the project evolve to a new-build scheme delivered in collaboration with local partners.

Rural Studio,
Hale County Animal Shelter, Greensboro,
Alabama,
2006

Education/construction/practice fusion Rural Studio create bespoke architectural solutions on behalf of the local community they work within. Here, four students from the practice arranged the finance, designed and ultimately constructed the shelter on behalf of Hale County which was without the means to provide the building.

Douglas Murphy

Constitutive Crises

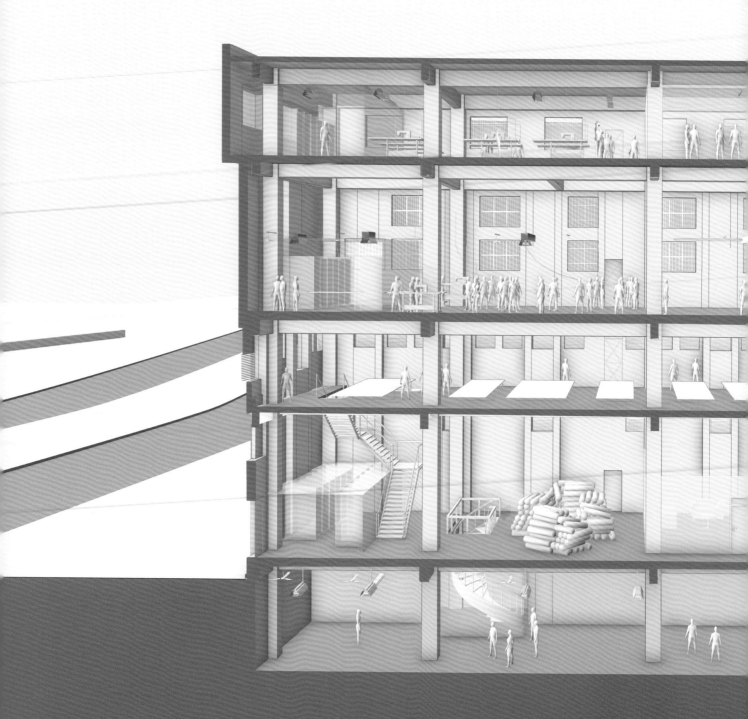

Radical Practice and the Definition of the Centre

Calls to reinvent architectural practice have been a steady part of the profession from its inception. Widely published cultural writer **Douglas Murphy**, who teaches in the architecture departments of the Royal College of Art and Central Saint Martins in London, tracks the variety of forms they have taken: from reactions to specific historical and technical developments, to perennial concerns regarding the architect's standing in society and on the building site.

Forensic Architecture, Outsourcing Risk: Investigating the Ali Enterprises Factory Fire on 11 September 2012, Goldsmiths, University of London, 2018

Forensic Architecture's interdisciplinary research team use professional expertise to assist investigations into conflict and disaster situations, such as its recent investigation into a 2012 Karachi garment factory fire that killed 260 people. Their work attempts to push architectural services into new fields of political engagement.

Today it is common to hear calls for the total reinvention of architectural practice, suggesting that the status quo is in a state of crisis. Architects as a profession are losing ground in the construction industry due to changes in information technology, while clients and builders are using contractual mechanisms to squeeze them out of the construction process. Architects are trained to provide spatial products that are no longer effective in the current world, are failing to challenge the location and modalities of spatial power, and to take advantage of the opportunities to exert political agency that they have as professionals.

Yet while it may appear that some of the challenges of the present day are unique to the time we are in, it is more difficult to find a period of time where architecture did *not* consider itself to be in a state of crisis than otherwise. But is it possible to separate anxieties that are constitutive of the profession from risks that are genuinely specific and urgent?

The architecture profession in the UK, as it stands today, is made up of just under 40,000 people.[1] There are roughly 7,000 architectural firms, of which more than half have 10 staff or fewer, and of which roughly 25 per cent are based in London.[2] The professional output of architects is mostly made up of house extensions. What this entails is that the community of people in focus when the architectural profession is discussed is only a few thousand strong.

The profession has terrible statistics for diversity. Despite making up around half of the student body, women make up only 26 per cent of the profession as a whole,[3] indicating a workplace environment distinctively hostile to gender equality. As well as predominantly male, the architecture profession is 95 per cent white, and architects tend to come from the middle classes, something that becomes even more pronounced as wages fail to keep up with rising costs of living.

One of the most common complaints is about the nature and quality of education. Objections range from pressing for the abolition of the Part II qualification, to criticism of the abstract nature of studio teaching and the relevance of the skills and techniques involved. As in many fields, there is a tension between questions of what can be taught in university that cannot be learned in the office, and the need for graduates ready for practice by the time they leave university.

Recent years have thrown up a number of apparent alternative methodologies for practice. These include collective practice, as demonstrated by collaborative London practice Assemble, who utilise craft and low-skill construction techniques to allow them to involve users and the public in their design processes, and whose multidisciplinary approach led to them winning the prestigious Turner Prize for fine art in 2015. Alongside them there are numerous young firms who, by aiming financially and technologically low, strive to bypass the more exploitative parts of the industry and engage more directly with communities.

Other approaches are more explicitly political, including organisations that blur the boundary between designers and campaigners. For example, Forensic Architecture – led by architect/academic Eyal Weizman at Goldsmiths, University of London and shortlisted for the 2018 Turner Prize – presents itself as a completely novel academic field, deploying expertise to highlight architecture's role in armed conflict, while Architects for Social Housing (ASH) is a London campaign group intervening directly in housing struggles through advice, advocacy and counter-proposal. Other alternatives include attempts to revive the role of the architect-planner, or even architect-developers who are able to work to different priorities than a standard developing client. Most of these approaches have been seen before, but have captured the imagination again, based upon the current experience of crisis.

Assemble,
Granby Four Streets,
Toxteth,
Liverpool,
2017

Assemble's work collaborating with a community land trust, social entrepreneur and local campaign groups brought 10 condemned houses back into use. Mixing methods of community architecture from previous generations with a collective artistic sensibility, work from this locally engaged project won Assemble the 2015 Turner Prize.

Crisis of Development

One of the earliest self-proclaimed architects in Britain was John Shute, who published the first English book on architecture, *The First and Chief Groundes of Architecture*, in 1563, after the Reformation. The rise of the Renaissance architect in Britain, as exemplified by Inigo Jones, marks a secularisation of the construction trade, and a cultivated interest coming from educated members of the upper classes. Through the publication of pattern books and other forms of knowledge transfer, Palladianism and other developments created conditions of taste and connoisseurship, and as construction technology was still relatively simple, architects could assert their worth by their ability to give form to the wealth and status of clients.

This new form of practice developed through the 17th century, although the activity of architects remained focused mainly on the upper classes and institutional clients. However, in the 18th century architecture began to be more greatly involved in the creation of multiple dwellings, and in some cases housing the poor, which marked a shift in the understanding of the role to society that an architect might play – rather than only representing and facilitating a certain kind of elite order in the world, a direct material intervention in the social project began to become apparent.

By the early 19th century the formation of architectural societies was the result of various crises formed and exacerbated through social change.[4] There was opportunity in building booms, such as those after the Napoleonic Wars, but aristocratic patronage was falling away, and upwardly mobile clients for domestic architecture were less likely to be experts in aesthetic theory. Architects found it difficult to protect their title from others, but also sensed unscrupulous behaviours were damaging their public profile. The Institute of British Architects was formed to represent the profession in 1834 and achieved royal charter a few years later, becoming the RIBA.

Many issues and complaints the RIBA worked through in these early years seem very familiar: exploitative competitions, London-centrism, and inconsistencies in training. Until the Architectural Association (AA) was formed in 1847, the only way to train as an architect was in the office of one. The radical early AA had allies in *The Builder*, founded in 1842, marking the appearance of a print/teaching axis, and their campaigning led the RIBA in 1887 to form a set of three professional examinations that has remained largely unchanged since.

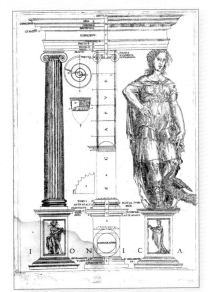

John Shute,
The First and Chief Groundes of Architecture, 1563

This was the first book published in English on the subject of architecture, featuring descriptions of the classical orders derived from Sebastiano Serlio's Italian *Seven Books of Architecture*.

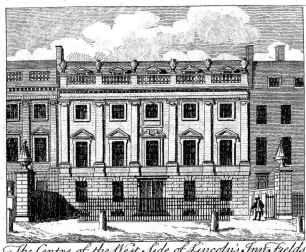

The Centre of the West Side of Lincoln's Inn Fields, late the Duke of Ancaster's, by Inigo Jones.

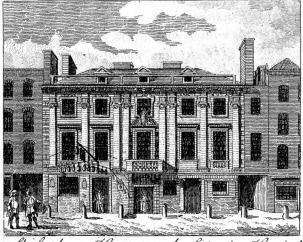

Shaftesbury House, now the Lying-in Hospital, by Inigo Jones.

Inigo Jones,
Lindsey House,
Lincoln's Inn Fields,
London,
1640,

Shaftesbury House,
Aldersgate,
London,
1644

The work of Jones represented a new kind of architectural practice in Britain, aligned to the aristocracy rather than the church, and producing high-taste design for educated patrons.

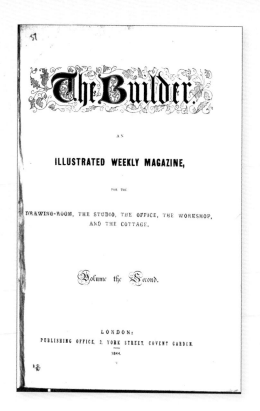

The Builder, 1844

The first architectural magazine in the UK began publication in 1842. Along with the Architectural Association (AA), it campaigned for reform in architectural education.

By the mid-1970s almost half of Britain's architects worked for local authorities, and between 1945 and 1975 they delivered nearly five million dwellings.[6] Postwar housing production peaked in 1968 with more than 400,000 dwellings being built, roughly half of which were council houses. One particular tension at this point related to just how radical the architectural production of local authorities was meant to be. On the one hand, the situation whereby purveyors of panel construction systems were able to reap government subsidy through building high was indeed a radically new path for the construction industry, but one that culminated in the fatal collapse in May 1968 of the 21-storey Ronan Point in Newham, East London, just two months after its opening, which brought discredit to the profession for generations.

Ronan Point,
Newham,
London,
May 1968

In May 1968, a gas explosion caused the progressive collapse of the 21-storey Ronan Point tower block, killing four people, just months after opening. The damage to the reputation of the architectural profession was long lasting.

The gentlemanly character of the profession was torn apart by the First World War, and then by the Great Depression, with one of the first mass redundancy crises. But overall the profession grew, and a new crisis began to loom as growing numbers of architects began to be employed in government as salaried workers, and had to fight to be recognised as a part of the profession as important as those in private practice.

In the interwar period, the 20th-century schism between Modernism and historicism began to make itself felt. Concerns about technology's effects on practice had already begun in the late 19th century, with the worry that engineers and builders were stealing work and monopolising new forms of knowledge while architects were otherwise distracted with the art of their endeavours. But interwar Modernism was still a minority position, treated with disdain, as in Edwin Lutyens's infamous 'The logic of a French mind may make a Corbusier house, or even a Versailles, but never a Hampton Court'.[5]

Crisis of Legitimacy

It would not be until after the trauma of the Second World War that a certain vision of the architect finally came into its own: the moulder of grand, socially binding visions of the city who demonstrated 'architecture or revolution'. The factors are simple: the huge amount of rebuilding that was required, a housing crisis that could no longer be ignored or downplayed, and an economic and political situation that gave power to democratic institutions such as planning departments.

But in celebrated cases, such as the London Borough of Camden Architects Department of the late 1960s, orthodoxy was radically challenged. This forward-facing milieu involved architects hired directly from universities being placed in positions of design control, and relied upon an architectural press that discussed and promoted conceptual ideas that were likely to be built; for example, Neave Brown could set out his case for 'The Form of Housing' in *D* in 1967,[7] as he – a Camden Council employee – designed the Fleet Road Estate that embodied those theories.

D,
September 1967

In the 1960s, *D* championed radical ideas from housing practice alongside Archigram and the 'Zoom' wave.

Neave Brown/London Borough of Camden Architects Department, Fleet Road Estate, Camden, London, 1966

Designed by Brown while an employee of Camden Council, the estate is a demonstration of a time in architecture when advanced design was congruent with academia and criticism.

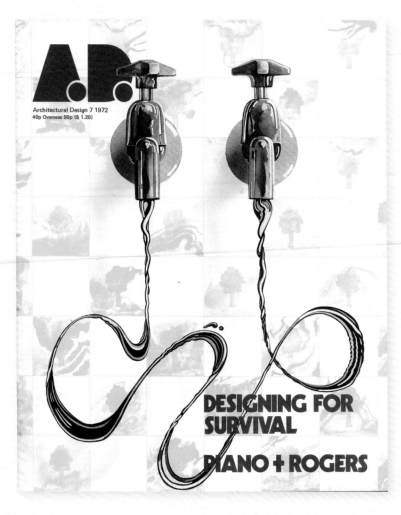

New Society, June 1966

The magazine *New Society*, first published in 1962, often featured radical ideas on architecture and the built environment, including Cedric Price's 'Potteries Thinkbelt', an attempt to completely rethink higher education.

The general fervour for 'progress' at this point, born of technological and social change, increasingly affected the architectural climate of the mid-1960s. Represented by figures such as Richard Buckminster Fuller and Cedric Price and various other more radical fringes such as Archigram and other 'Zoom' designers, a new form of utopianism attempted to agitate for the total transformation of building within the political parameters at the time. Much of this energy was found in the universities, and in the UK a large part of this trend was located at the AA.

The architectural press was another major field for this kind of debate. Magazines such as the *Architectural Review* and *Architects' Journal* could be seen to be maintaining a position that represented the profession as a whole, whereas a magazine such as *AD*, under the editorship of Monica Pidgeon, took a far more radical position, promoting experimental and conceptual work, publishing themed issues on ecology and cybernetics, and featuring writers such as Reyner Banham, Martin Pawley and Royston Landau, all arguing that the architectural profession was dangerously behind the times.

AD would, after the radical technology movement ran out of energy in the aftermath of the oil crisis of 1973, put its weight behind Postmodernism, which reacted on a number of levels to both what had been the status quo in practice, but also the grand claims being made for radical architecture at that point. The house-building boom was over, growth was focused on suburbs rather than inner cities, and a transition to a new phase of capitalism was underway.

AD, July 1972

While other magazines remained more closely aligned to the profession, *AD* featured cybernetics, ecology and radical politics.

The professional response to this particular crisis was varied. In some cases the new political reality was welcomed, and some architects argued specifically for the jettisoning of a politically inflected view of practice in favour of letting the market decide, essentially returning to the bourgeois situation of centuries previously. Another shift in terrain was towards academic and paper architecture, represented by the work of *Oppositions Journal*, based in New York and published between 1973 and 1984, where British intellectuals such as Kenneth Frampton and Alan Colquhoun could find like-minds such as Peter Eisenman and an associated academic ecosystem of Ivy League architecture departments.

Back in the UK, architects on the left who were unable to stomach the new climate of public hostility, led by Prince Charles, were sometimes able to move into community architecture, completing small-scale and low-paid work for inner-city communities that were suffering greatly in the 1980s, or they could – like Martin Pawley – keep faith in the architecture of the likes of Norman Foster and Richard Rogers, the 'British High Tech' that indeed carried the day after an enthusiastic commissioning spree after the end of the Thatcher era.

In academia, Alvin Boyarsky becoming head of the AA in 1971 at a time of serious financial crisis marked the end of the era of big-name Modernist teachers, and the coming into its own of the unit system. It is not hard to see this as a symptom of the financial turn in politics, as existing conflicts between egos and approaches were cultivated as the fuel of teaching, and conscious variety set off an individualistic system of competition that gave rise to many of the 'starchitects', such as Zaha Hadid or Rem Koolhaas, who would become globally successful in the early 2000s.

The unit system was developed even further by Archigram's Peter Cook, who was head of the Bartlett School of Architecture at University College London (UCL) from 1990 to 2005. Cook pushed an ethos whereby architectural education became something so impressive, so comprehensive and so creative that being an architect was perhaps the least interesting thing that could be done with it: 'relish those who move outside conventional so-called "practice"', he said, 'their books, films, exhibitions, or chairs still have much to say about architecture'.[8]

This idea that architecture was somehow a unique holistic education teaching 'intelligence and intuition, creativity and invention, dissection and synthesis, interpretation and speculation, problem-spotting and solving, rigour and obsession, and the courage and independence to enquire, take risks and be unpredictable'[9] not only neatly echoes the Renaissance ideal, but reflected another crisis, whereby young architects could no longer dream of taking their academic project directly into practice, and instead experienced the jarring transition from conceptual work to commercial drudgery, a situation that created conditions of disillusionment that helped drive some of the alternative practices mentioned earlier that emerged after the 2008 financial crisis.

Crisis to Come?

Any attempt to look at challenges in the future has to recognise worries that have been more or less constant over time. Fear about the quality and control of architectural education has been there since the beginning, as has the fear of losing the place at the main meeting table, while the anxiety over contemporary technology has been present since the Industrial Revolution. In their own way, these worries can be seen as being part of what constitutes the profession, which implies that at any given point those setting off for new kinds of practice are in fact helping to define where the centre is actually located.

But nothing is permanent, and in the current situation there are some easily discerned risks and challenges coming up. The contractual muscling that began in the 1980s with the import of 'design-and-build' contracts continues, and in many cases architects have been forced to retreat to being little more than intermediaries between clients and planning departments.

As construction technology – within both the building and the design process – becomes yet more sophisticated, the ability to knowledgeably control an entire project recedes yet further. The Grenfell Tower fire of 2017 demonstrated just how complex supply chains and contractual responsibilities have become, and how difficult it is to discern responsibilities within them.

Automation may pose a threat to many more technical roles in practice, killing off jobs, but this occurs at a time when more and more architects are being trained, raising the possibility of a massive oversupply in coming years.

The way in which discussion takes place is changing as well, as architectural print magazines die at the same time as a boom in comment through social media has occurred. It is not inconceivable that the self-fashioning of the discipline through discursive media could itself wither.

On top of all this, current political and ecological risks promise to render any predictions ludicrous. But at the very least, in order to survive, architecture will have to continue similarly reinventing itself way into the future. ⌂

Notes
1. 38,511 in 2016 according to the Architects Registration Board (ARB), 'ARB's Annual Report 2016': http://2016.arb.org.uk/.
2. Office for National Statistics, 'Architecture and Architects in London and the UK', 7 February 2017: www.ons.gov.uk/employmentandlabourmarket/peopleinwork/employmentandemployeetypes/adhocs/006620architectureandarchitectsinlondonandtheuk.
3. Architects Registration Board, *op cit*.
4. Angela Mace, *The Royal Institute of British Architects: A Guide to its Archive and History*, Mansell (London), 1986, p xiv.
5. Edwin Lutyens, 'The Robotism of Architecture', reprinted in *RIBA Journal*, 115 (9), September 2008, pp 22–3.
6. Stefan Muthesius and Miles Glendinning, *Tower Block: Modern Public Housing in England, Scotland, Wales and Northern Ireland*, Yale University Press (New Haven, CT), 1994, pp 331–2.
7. Neave Brown, 'The Form of Housing', *Architectural Design*, September 1967, p 432.
8. Peter Cook in Laura Allen (ed), *Bartlett Works: Architecture, Buildings, Projects*, August Projects (London), 2004.
9. Iain Borden in Allen, *op cit*.

Shumi Bose

**DIVERSICATION
OF THE ROLE**

Financing the Expanded Field

Adding Value Through Innovative Practice

THE ECONOMIST BUILDING

0 2 MAY 2017

Is the architect's role primarily creative, commercial or service-based? And what economic opportunities can be opened up by embracing more than one of these categories? London-based teacher, curator and editor **Shumi Bose** looks at the multiple different ways qualified architects can earn a living in these financially challenging times. Highlighting examples from theory and practice on both sides of the Atlantic, she examines the options – from entrepreneurship to academia and from specialisation to diversification – and explores how some practitioners are making the most of new media and modes of collaboration.

The traditional role of the architect is shrinking, constrained through the operations of economy, policy, building technologies and myriad other factors. Efficiently automated and stripped away into separate industries, the loss of exclusive domain over a specific activity offers little security in terms of billed hours. As Charles Holland writes in 'The Economies of Architecture': 'the resulting diversification, while offering a creative dynamic, also mirrors the fragmentation of an increasingly competitive marketplace.'[1]

At the same time, the opportunity to exercise creative, ethical and artistic freedoms appears to be pushing certain practitioners to extend the field of architectural practice into roles of social and community engagement, policy and governance, research, activism and art practice. Although this hardly constitutes a majority of the professional sphere, those who are successful in expanding the field are often fêted as demonstrating a new agency for the discipline.

Yet, without taking away from the success of individual initiatives, or diminishing the generosity of intent, there are important questions that should form part of the emergent expanded discourse. Firstly, whether such an 'expansion' is appropriate – if the practice of architecture is, in other words, a service industry, a creative field or a commercial enterprise. More prosaically, perhaps, is whether such expansion is fungible; whether the expanded remit leads to an increase in value in terms of architects' labour and remuneration.

A 2017 article in the *RIBA Journal* paints a complex but distinctly un-rosy picture for architects, with average earnings, when adjusted for consumer inflation, down between 12 and 16 per cent (albeit with a nominal increase between 2016 and 2017).[2] High susceptibility to inflation leaves architects exposed, and the low growth in nominal terms means that even rises in fees, however unlikely in terms of increased competition, may not comfortably bolster professional earnings. To bear this out in historical real terms, the average (male) architect's salary has increased less than 7 per cent since 1977, while the median male worker's salary has increased by a quarter.

From self-initiated projects, to those architects who have found more room to manoeuvre on the fringes of an increasingly variegated discipline, the extent to which architects are able to exercise agency is constrained only by the financial and strategic realities of practice. Here lies the problem of inequitable aspiration; in order to function in the 'expanded' field of socially engaged or artistic practice, for example, practitioners need a degree of financial independence or agility that would allow for the pursuit of non-commercial endeavours. How do architects find a viable way to operate without the support of commercial mechanisms? What are the economics of an expanded field?

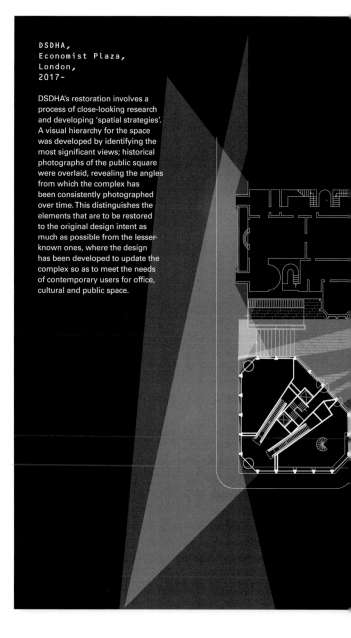

How do architects find a viable way to operate without the support of commercial mechanisms? What are the economics of an expanded field?

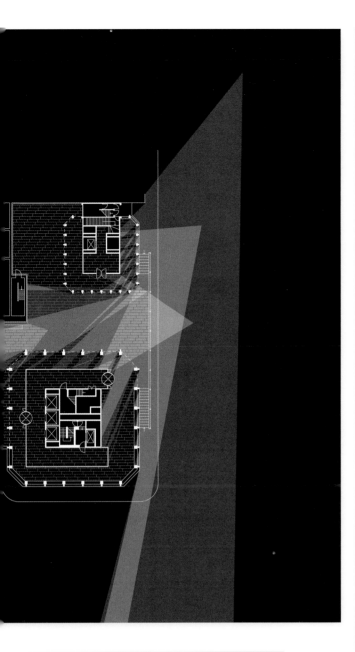

Marks Barfield Architects,
British Airways i360,
Brighton,
UK,
2016

This vertical cable car on Brighton's seafront by David Marks and Julia Barfield, the architects of the London Eye, is testimony to the couple's belief in the regenerative power of architecture: the tower stands on the site of Brighton's derelict West Pier. It is also a reflection of their tenacity as they took on the financial risk of the scheme, leading on the speculative development of the structure as well as its design.

Works or Labour?

Following the Renaissance focus on *disegno*, Jon Goodbun and Karin Jaschke name drawings as the primary production of architects – that which, according to the professional definition, should provide direct and definite compensation. However, 'because of the capability of architects to produce drawings without significant capital outlay,' they argue, 'the drawing is in no way responsible for architects to engage in large amounts of unpaid or low paid speculative work.'[3] As related technologies, practices and sub-industries evolve to produce renders, animations and visualisations, and furthermore as such processes are at least partially automated through digital and computational modelling, this tendency is only exacerbated. Only when the drawing receives the status of an artwork can the value potentially exceed the cost of labour.

Goodbun and Jaschke's formulation, recalling Hannah Arendt's distinction between work and labour,[4] is not untimely. A focus on the nature of work would serve to speculate on the possibility for design, design value, collaboration, procurement, retention and accreditation. How do we measure architectural work, or works in the production and distribution of (abstract and concrete) artefacts, or by revenues generated through a specific pursuit?

Make Something of Yourself: Entrepreneurialism

Entrepreneurialism is perhaps the red thread of the collected 'strategies' gathered in this piece; the entrepreneurial is in learning to value each part of architectural practice as a chargeable service that would sustain a business. Such an approach therefore runs through the core of all 'extended' professional activities. Deborah Saunt of DSDHA, for example, claims that her PhD process allowed her to recognise research as the primary, and potentially most valuable, production of the office, altering the performance and review of the practice output as a whole.[5] Offering research and 'spatial strategy' as a chargeable service has led to non-traditional projects, which would give the office greater resilience should building projects ever thin out, as they have done over the economic volatilities of the past decade. Continuing on a pragmatic level, the creation of a distinct 'research entity' within the practice business structure means that research funding, often hard-won through lengthy and soul-searching grant application processes, can be allocated and protected rather than being all too easily absorbed by the costs of running an office.

Younger firms can also be seen to be using entrepreneurial tactics more often seen in art practice, advertising and branding, demonstrating savvy attitudes to evaluating value, but also a hunger to develop managerial strategies, maintaining teams, business awareness and collaborative networks. The urgency behind some of these moves is due to a major oversight in education. According to Holly Lewis of We Made That (see also her article on pp 110–15 of this issue): 'Nobody in the first six years of education told us that you could run your own practice.'[6]

As financialised as our schools and universities may be, the notion of financial management and how to value architectural labour is one area sorely underplayed in the curriculum, much to the disadvantage of graduates. Pedagogically speaking, this would suggest expanding not only the field of professional practice, but in parallel expanding the parochial horizons of professional practice education to include entrepreneurialism.

Adding Value: Academic Practice

A study by Silke Ötsch, conducted across several cities in the UK, Austria, France and the US, found that young architects in particular suffered from this professional diversification.[7] Unsurprisingly, perhaps, it found that architects' incomes are frequently supplemented by advisory services, entrepreneurialism in the cultural and (more lucratively) in the real-estate sector, and by university teaching – the most accessible and intellectually respectable option of 'expanded' practice.

The exchange between pedagogy and practice has long been one of the most fruitful and professionally rewarding activities. For students and practitioners to be alongside each other is in the ancient tradition of the guilds, wherein knowledge is both subtly and explicitly passed from master to pupil. School faculties boast the extent to which curriculum is delivered by 'active practitioners', allowing students the benefit of working with those whose mettle is proven in commercial terms, gaining not only scholarly and technical skills, but real-world nous. The arrangement is mutually beneficial, as practitioners can use the studio as a laboratory, setting tasks which parallel their predilections or professional challenges. As a corollary, trends show that more architecture graduates work within architecture now and in the previous six years than ever before.[8]

The academy allows that which the profession may not; the possibility to explore experimental and critical investigations, strengthening the case for practitioners who teach as an essential aspect of professional and personal development. To cite another, perhaps more crucial advantage, the academy offers a buffer of income, almost always modest, but blissfully regular, which allows many architects, without mincing words, to survive. It can be a devil's bargain, though; that free laboratory comes with extremely demanding rats, whose high fees cause them to be increasingly so. Although the pay may be regular, in the UK it is often very low, and comes with attendant paperwork that can drown all possibility of pursuing a professional 'design' practice during those unpaid hours or days.

Zone In: Specialisation

If more of architects' traditional operation can be specialised out, it follows that when the lens is reversed, an architectural education is diverse enough that its skills are applicable and beneficial when applied to other sectors. There are obvious synergies between architectural visualisation and computer graphics, animation and game development; the functions of virtual reality environments are extending through educational to therapeutic industries. The technical expertise developed by the office of Marks Barfield, for example, has been deployed by the firm in many other urban proposals,

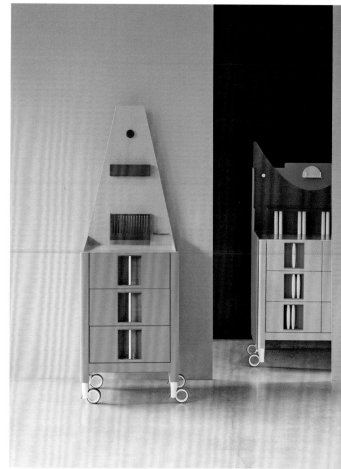

Adam Nathaniel Furman,
Gateways,
London,
2017

above: These four highly coloured tiled gateways, sponsored by Turkish Ceramics, in Granary Square at the centre of King's Cross, formed the decorative entranceway to the 'Design Junction' show during the 2017 London Design Festival.

Adam Nathaniel Furman,
Nakano Twins,
2018

opposite: This duo of flamboyant cartoon-like cabinets cleverly simulate the anime shops in Tokyo's Nakano Broadway, which sell video games, manga and animation, while also reviving the most colourful and joyous spirit of 1980s Postmodernism redolent of Milan's Memphis Group.

ultimately initiating the British Airways i360 project in Brighton (2016), now the world's first vertical moving observation tower.

On the other hand, architectural 'systems thinking' is increasingly valued at the level of urban planning and governance. The remarkable specialisation of young practice We Made That allows for laudable credibility in a particular field: over 95 per cent of its projects are with public authority clients, embodying its claim to a strong spirit of public conscience. The practice's first project (A Hut for Gazing and Canoodling, Lincolnshire, 2010) was an audacious competition win with a public authority; following this, co-founders Holly Lewis and Oliver Goodhall cultivated clients and relationships in this sector by choice. It is worth noting that this specialisation was only possible thanks to supportive employers before the pair were financially stable enough to strike out on their own, underlining the important tradition of nurturing young practitioners within the profession. As a result, and by the time they did so, they attained a position of expertise and a portfolio of experience in working with the public sector.

Punch Harder, Engage Wider: Collaboration

Architecture is inherently a collaborative profession; its value is in orchestrating and visioning the interplay between multiple skeins of knowledge and understanding. Harnessing these diverse relationships – with manufacturers, larger practices, as consultants and co-authors – can lead to different tiers of exposure, and help to build a client base. A strategic way of thinking about the benefits of collaboration is as a means to get into rooms where one otherwise might not be invited. As Lewis has reflected, collaboration can be a point of departure for ambition. Following substantial collaborations with the London School of Economics and the office of the Mayor of London among others, We Made That sees collaborative practice as a cavalier advantage: 'How far above our weight can we punch?'[9]

Through written, material and historical research, Adam Nathaniel Furman has developed not only his own highly individual design aesthetic, but also a position of authority on the subject of Postmodernism. Most effectively, a clever use of social media has created awareness and engagement, as well as wider recognition for his research – the swell of engagement was undoubtedly underlined and validated by his collaboration with celebrated architect Terry Farrell, eventually leading to co-authorship of a significant and authoritative publication.[10] Furman also claims that choosing the nomenclature of designer allows for more flexibility in terms of a field of operation. Operating fluidly within the art and design world, his promiscuous collaborations with commercial Turkish Ceramics and *Wallpaper** allow for a prolific production of installations and objects, and a level of visibility highly desirable for a young designer.

Take a Risk: Diversification

There seems to be little consensus, parity or acuity in measuring the value of the architect viz the value of a project; for built works, the duration of involvement, location and clear discrepancies between ground-up and refurbishment. A crude averaging of the 2017 'AJ Fees Survey'[11] would demonstrate that most architects receive less than 9 per cent of the value of built projects. Might it be possible to strengthen that percentage through diversification?

Growing numbers believe that integrating part of the procurement and building process – rather than novation to an arguably dispensable advisory role – is a way of retaining design quality as well as value. But many firms would find it difficult to insist on such conditions within a larger structure of procurement. In the US, firms such as SHoP Architects advocate for less stigma around the architect-developer model. In 1971, the American Institute of Architects (AIA) revoked its once-held fear that the crassness of commerce would overtake the architect's professional sensibilities, and even issued a document encouraging architects to pursue property development.

As common argument holds, developers make greater gains due to greater risks, so if you want real skin in the game – as well as greater design, procurement and ethical control – one way is to retain a financial interest as developer, even as part of a consortium. Speaking to the *Architects' Journal*, Sophie Goldhill of Liddicoat & Goldhill says: 'The industry will need to adapt or die. Acting as developer is one way of reclaiming territory for the architect, and a great way of improving the prospects for the quality of our built environment.'[12] However, most small practices have limited capital, and would likely be stretched to support further liabilities; it would undoubtedly be challenging for cash-poor architects to enter the domain of the developer. The availability of land is also problematic, especially for urban practices. Yet if there are improved legal vehicles for consensus, it may be possible for architects to act as stakeholders within collective models.

Through the increased popularity and interest in community land trust (CLT) models and collective custom build, architects might find opportunities to offer services in a way that differs from traditional architect–client relationships. This entails being prepared to take the risk of a different kind of relationship with a collective client rather than a single client, which in turn has significant decision-making, liability and potentially fee-impacting implications.

SHoP Architects,
325 Kent,
Brooklyn,
New York,
2018

Having gained an understanding of property development from the inside, SHoP are now working at a colossal scale in Brooklyn with developers Two Trees. The practice is the masterplanner of the Domino Sugar Refinery site at Williamsburg, which includes a total of 2,800 apartments, and a significant waterfront park designed by James Corner Field Operations. 325 Kent is the first completed building with 522 rental apartments, including 100 units at affordable below-market rents.

SHoP Architects,
The Porter House,
New York,
2003

SHoP gained their first major breakthrough project in New York by initiating their own development, the restoration of an early 20th-century warehouse into condominiums in the then up-and-coming Meatpacking District.

Facit Homes,
Graven Hill,
near Bicester,
Oxfordshire,
UK,
2018

above: Graven Hill is the largest custom-build site in the UK with 1,900 homes planned. Driven by a development company set up by the local Cherwell District Council, it offers plots for sale for self-build and custom build. Facit Homes is providing individually designed and digitally manufactured homes made in an East London factory. Clad with a mix of corten steel and timber, this five-bedroom house has a digitally manufactured Facit-designed chassis timber structure.

below: By using adaptable designs with light flexible spaces, Facit Homes is able to offer a bespoke service for home buyers at Graven Hill. This open-plan interior has triple-glazed bi-fold doors to the rear and strip roof lighting over the kitchen area.

If architecture is to be considered one of 'the professions' – defined by a long and specifically prescribed course of education – it is a weak one.

Untying the Gordian Knot

If architecture is to be considered one of 'the professions' – defined by a long and specifically prescribed course of education – it is a weak one. Neither medical nor legal practices have nor can be systematised, industrialised, digitised and commodified to the extent of the built environment.[13] None of the 'strategies' above are new, or exclusively contemporary conditions enabled by the present moment. The architectural profession has been trying to justify itself since its formal conception in the 15th century. The particular pressure or difficulty for some architects in supporting themselves through the core business of design practice is, however, a contemporary exacerbation and necessarily unprecedented; this derives variously from advancements towards automation in building information technology, from the extreme financialisation of construction, and not least from the internally questioning culture of the discipline itself.

Returning to Arendt's formulation, if labour is repetitive, never-ending, under submission, done out of necessity, then work is instrumental, temporally defined, enduring, result-producing.[14] In architecture, labour is conducted by a salaried workforce in order to articulate and achieve 'work', but architects are regarded for 'works' – as specific artefacts – rather than for the collective pursuits entailed in labour. Might this be the root of its baffling and precarious asymmetries as a profession? Perhaps the weak profession, precisely due to its ability to compound multiple functions in a Gordian knot, can be seen as resilient; crucially, when untangled, the multi-stranded labour of architecture must be valued along its full extent. ⌀

Notes

1. Charles Holland, 'The Economies of Architecture', *Perspecta 47: Money*, August 2014, p 160.
2. Brian Green, 'Rises But No Shine', *RIBA Journal*, 14 November 2017: www.ribaj.com/intelligence/market-analysis-average-architects-earnings.
3. Jon Goodbun and Karin Jaschke, 'Means of (Re-)production: Fame and the Changing Role of the Drawing', in Paul Davies and Torsten Schmiedeknecht (eds), *An Architect's Guide to Fame: A Collection of Essays on Why They Got Famous and You Didn't*, Routledge (London), 2005, p 59.
4. See, for example, Hannah Arendt, *The Human Condition*, University of Chicago Press (Chicago, IL), 1958, especially pp 79–90.
5. In conversation with the author, DSDHA offices, London, 1 February 2018.
6. See the podcast posted by Business of Architecture, 'Young and Accomplished: A Conversation with Holly Lewis of We Made That', 26 May 2017: www.youtube.com/watch?v=YFaFn4Po8e8.
7. Silke Ötsch, 'The Architect: A Disappearing Species in a Financialized Space?', in Juliet Odgers, Mhairi McVicar and Stephen Kite (eds), *Economy and Architecture*, Routledge (London), 2016, pp 162–74.
8. On average, 80 per cent of students graduating in Architecture between 2011 and 2016 are in full-, part-time or self-employment (a further 18 per cent are in higher education). Of the employed majority, 83 per cent of these are working in architecture. Source: RIBA Student Destination Survey 2016: www.architecture.com/-/media/gathercontent/riba-student-destinations-survey/additional-documents/reportribastudentdestinationssurvey2016pdf.pdf.
9. In conversation with the author, London School of Economics, 5 December 2017.
10. Terry Farrell and Adam Nathaniel Furman, *Revisiting Postmodernism*, RIBA Publishing (Newcastle upon Tyne), 2017.
11. Richard Waite, 'AJ Fees Survey 2017: How Much Are You Charging?', *Architects' Journal*, 244 (10), 2017, pp 6–8.
12. Richard Waite, Colin Marrs and Laura Mark, 'Who Wants to be an Architect/Developer?', *Architects' Journal*, 243 (2), 2016, pp 10–13.
13. This definition of weak professionality has been expounded by Mark Cousins, longstanding educator at the Architectural Association (AA), in conversation with the author, and in lectures to second-year students at the AA: 'The Renaissance and the Classical Tradition', 13 October 2016 and 'The Life and Death of Architecture', 2 March 2017.
14. Arendt, *op cit*, pp 79–90.

Alison Killing

Building Digital Stories

Architecture and Cartography Meet Documentary and Journalism

Architects' skills of spatial analysis and representation can be put to good use in surprisingly diverse fields. In the case of **Alison Killing**, whose studio Killing Architects is based in Rotterdam, they serve to raise public awareness and understanding of topical issues such as migration and climate change. She reveals what motivated her to branch out in this direction, describes a recent self-initiated project in detail, and notes how the Netherlands' well-known culture of encouraging designers to pursue research has helped.

In 2011, European architecture research collective Wonderland released its *Manual for Emerging Architects*,[1] a survey of young practices from across the continent. As the basis for offering advice to those hoping to follow in the footsteps of these firms, it catalogued their workloads, the financial viability of their practice, and the proportion of their work that comprised construction as opposed to teaching, research and other activities considered tangential to the traditional role of architects. Crucially, it did not assume that building buildings would be the only, or even default activity of these practices. This state of otherness was viewed mostly as a function of their youth and creativity rather than other external factors such as the economy.

The manual was an instructive place to start thinking about future possibilities for the architecture profession because it caught those it featured at a critical early stage, at pivotal points when they may not yet have built that first building that would prove their competence to future clients, nor have the turnover to allow them to participate in tendering for work, forcing them to look more widely for opportunities. Also revealing is the support for these other activities, in the form of public grant funding or institutions that might host events and exhibitions, which shapes the opportunities available for young practices and from there, the future direction offices are able to take. The study was remarkable in its openness to what the practice of architecture could be, its Europe-wide vision less at risk of being limited by the specific constraints imposed on practice in any given country.

It is interesting to set a 2011 Royal Institute of British Architects (RIBA) funded report on the future of architecture against this. Like the Wonderland survey, *The Future for Architects?*[2] was published as part of RIBA's Building Futures programme a couple of years into the financial crisis, which was having a particularly devastating effect on the construction sector. It also hinged on a fairly specific, quite traditional understanding of what architectural practice is, even if some of those interviewed expressed vague ambitions of moving beyond this. Its jumping-off point was how the role of architects had diminished over the preceding decades, supplanted in the construction process by engineers, quantity surveyors and project managers. It then projected this pattern into the future, envisaging a world of large corporate practices and small boutiques, and little in between. It painted a depressing picture at a depressing time, but also a deeply reactive one, in stark contrast to Wonderland's broader, more positive approach.

Killing Architects was founded in Rotterdam in 2010 and belongs firmly to the cohort that Wonderland surveyed rather than the more established firms that were the focus of the RIBA report. The practice's decision to move from building towards applying its architectural skills elsewhere was not made quickly, or even, at first, deliberately. Established at the height of the economic crisis, there was little construction activity and few jobs to bid for, especially for young architects. At the same time, it was no coincidence that the Wonderland study had found architects in the Netherlands, where there is public funding for designers to pursue research and a strong ecosystem of museums and design institutions to support this more theoretical work, to have the greatest proportion of their workload come from non-building projects. The practice's focus on work beyond construction was therefore a combination of these push-and-pull factors.

The core of its work has been communicating to non-specialists how the built environment functions, through writing, exhibitions, film and research. Many of the larger issues we currently face as a society, such as irregular migration[3] and climate change, have a strong spatial component. Though there is interest from the architecture profession in engaging with these problems, as evidenced by the regular design competitions and student proposals addressing, for example, shelter for refugees, they are usually treated only as opportunities for largely unnecessary design interventions. There is often an unwillingness to acknowledge that the main solutions to these issues may lie beyond the realm of the design, in the policies that shape migration and asylum border control, and that there are other ways in which architects' skills can be relevant. Their ability to analyse and represent spatial information, for example, can support the work of those, such as journalists and documentary makers, trying to communicate these important issues, and it is this direction that the practice's work has recently started to explore.

Where Architecture Meets Documentary

Migration trail is a 10-day-long online experience that joins a Nigerian man and a Syrian woman a little way into their journeys as they set off from North Africa and Turkey, travelling to and through Europe, in real time via an animated mapped data visualisation. For ethical reasons it is a reconstruction, but presented as live in order to convey the urgency and immediacy of the events. The audience can follow the two characters on the map within the visualisation, their voices presented as a 10-day 'instant messaging feed' by professional writers from Nigeria and Lebanon. A daily podcast explores the wider issues.

The project has two aims – to create a better-informed discussion about migration to Europe, and to show that a compelling story can be told using data and maps. Like much of Killing Architects' work, migration trail is a self-initiated project funded through research, documentary and design grants, in this case from the Creative Industries Fund NL, Netherlands Film Fund, Dutch Media Fund and Arts Council England, as part of a The Space/WIRED Creative Innovation Fellowship.

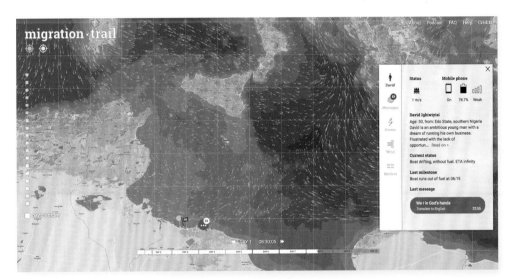

Killing Architects,
The central Mediterranean,
migration trail,
2017

The central Mediterranean between Libya and Italy is a key migration route from North Africa to Europe. The wind data shown on the map is important because of its effect in generating waves that pose a serious risk to the unseaworthy boats typically used for this journey.

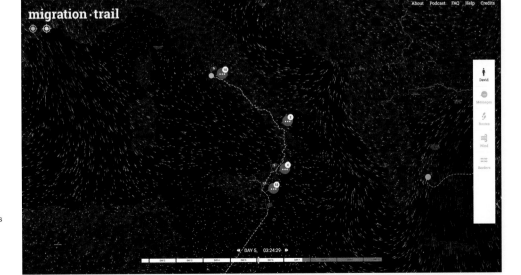

Killing Architects,
Night view of Europe,
migration trail,
2017

The route of one of the characters followed in the migration trail data visualisation. The message icons on the map indicate the position at which an instant message was sent.

Killing Architects,
Turkey and Lesbos,
migration trail,
2017

The route of the Syrian character
followed in the migration trail
data visualisation, from Izmir
in Turkey to Lesbos, Greece.

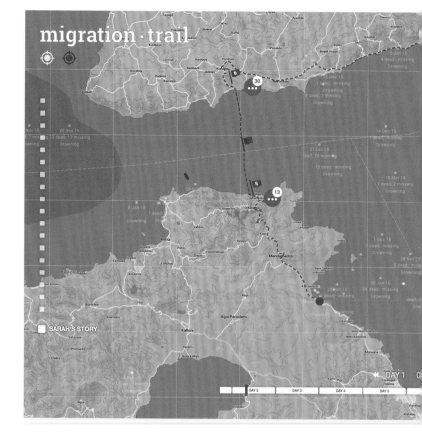

There was clearly room for
another approach to the story.
Telling it via a map, in real
time, could bring urgency and
immediacy to a problem that
was going largely ignored.

Killing Architects,
Night view of central Athens,
migration trail,
2017

The colours of the map change
as it moves from day to night.

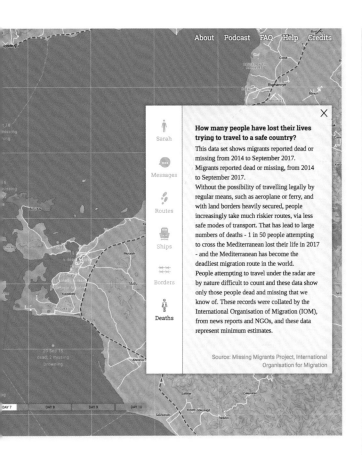

How many people have lost their lives trying to travel to a safe country?

This data set shows migrants reported dead or missing from 2014 to September 2017. Migrants reported dead or missing, from 2014 to September 2017.

Without the possibility of travelling legally by regular means, such as aeroplane or ferry, and with land borders heavily secured, people increasingly take much riskier routes, via less safe modes of transport. That has lead to large numbers of deaths - 1 in 50 people attempting to cross the Mediterranean lost their life in 2017 - and the Mediterranean has become the deadliest migration route in the world.

People attempting to travel under the radar are by nature difficult to count and these data show only those people dead and missing that we know of. These records were collated by the International Organisation of Migration (IOM), from news reports and NGOs, and these data represent minimum estimates.

Source: Missing Migrants Project, International Organisation for Migration

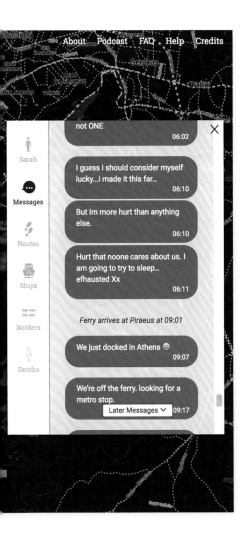

Many previous attempts to build online documentaries and storytelling projects using maps over the past few years have met with limited success. Specific challenges have included a lack, until relatively recently, of the software and graphic interfaces required to work more intuitively to create the required cartography, with one of the only options being to build on Google Maps. Copyright issues have restricted what creators could do. The Google platform did not permit users to change colours, or to distort the map in any way, inhibiting the range of information that could be communicated given the importance of visually highlighting what an audience should focus on and how they interpret what they see. In addition, existing platforms mostly revolved around pinning photos, videos and text to a map. This gave the material some geographic context, but visually lacked the structure to guide viewers in terms of what to look at and in what sequence in order to build a narrative. After a first prototype using Google, the migration trail team moved on to a custom system built using Leaflet, an open-source JavaScript library, with map information from OpenStreetMap and styling carried out in Mapbox, a strategy which allowed the necessary flexibility.

Although media coverage gathered pace from 2015, when Killing Architects first began work on the migration trail project in the autumn of 2014 the migration issue was attracting relatively little interest despite the large numbers of people crossing the central Mediterranean and a series of shocking capsizings, shipwrecks and attendant deaths. There was clearly room for another approach to the story. Telling it via a map, in real time, could bring urgency and immediacy to a problem that was going largely ignored.

Migration is also complicated and poorly understood, making it difficult for readers of news reports to join individual events together into a coherent narrative, partly because the events are geographically disparate (and therefore often lack obvious connections), and also because news journalism is inherently fragmentary. In migration trail, structuring this narrative around a journey provides a framework for understanding how the different chapters – tales of Libyan smugglers, Hungarian border closures and camp evictions in Calais – are all part of the same, larger story.

The migration trail map structure lends itself well to providing the context for individual stories as well as showing the links between them, and the zoom level offers a further structuring mechanism. Zooming in reveals personal data about individual migrant characters, such as the availability of wifi in their vicinity, or how far they can continue to travel before their phone battery will run out. Zoom out and the map shows statistics and other information that put the journey into context; for example, the relative strength of different countries' passports measured by how much visa-free travel they afford their holder, or where asylum seekers make claims in Europe and how likely their claims are to be granted in different countries. The zoom mechanism therefore links the small-scale and personal to the large-scale context.

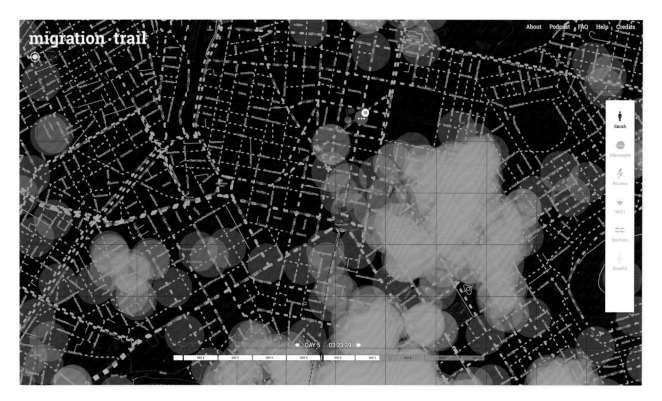

In migration trail user testing sessions, people inevitably zoomed in on their own country first, to find out where the refugees were, how much money the state had promised to give, and how much it had actually given.

Killing Architects,
Wifi availability in Athens,
migration trail,
2017

Potential public wifi availability in central Athens. Internet access is essential for people on the move to stay in touch with friends and family, as well as for planning the journey.

Killing Architects,
Passport strength,
migration trail,
2017

The strength of different countries' passports ranked by how much visa-free travel they afford their holders. The difficulty of obtaining a visa often bars people from safe, regular forms of transport forcing them into risky, irregular journeys. Data source: Passport Index.

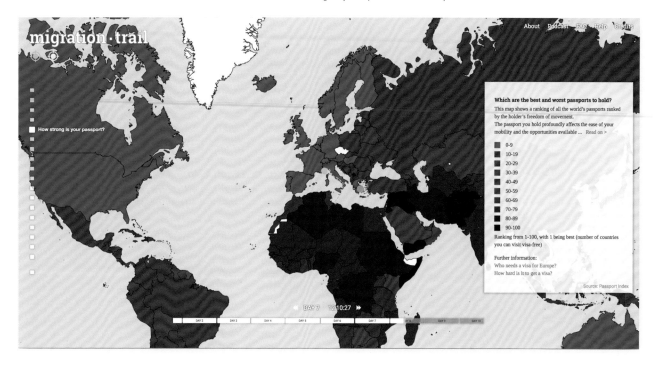

As the project developed, other lessons emerged regarding how people use maps. Though maps and data might at first seem abstract, they can also be very powerful in personalising a story and showing how it relates to an individual viewer. In migration trail user testing sessions, people inevitably zoomed in on their own country first, to find out where the refugees were, how much money the state had promised to give, and how much it had actually given. They were searching for their place in the story in a very literal way, and from there, trying to understand how the rest of the information related to them. Maps and data thus turned out to be much more personal than had been anticipated at the outset.

Killing Architects,
World employment rates,
migration trail,
2017

Large-scale map showing statistics that help to put the individual journeys into context. Employment rates were one of the factors used to calculate the EU's relocation quotas for how many refugees individual states should take. Data source: International Labour Organization.

Transferable Skills

A background in architecture proved essential in developing migration trail, but the need for this skill set on a project that could be described, probably with greater accuracy, as journalism and documentary is not self-evident. Part of the reason Killing Architects was able to successfully engage with it was the office's unusually broad experience, for example in humanitarianism and development, which was key for the work on irregular migration. There was also a clear need for technical drawing and visual communication skills to execute the maps. The more broadly transferable skill that architects bring, however, is design, which though typically applied to buildings, is agnostic regarding subject matter.

Migration trail would also not have been possible without close collaborations with colleagues from other fields, drawing a parallel with the interdisciplinary nature of traditional construction projects. Working with people from different backgrounds is powerful in allowing us to do more than any of us could do alone, but inevitably involves a loss of purity, the blurring of disciplines and the adoption of some of our skills and knowledge by others. So while we may continue to find new applications, conversely we may always be in the position of needing to rethink our role and reinvent ourselves. ⌂

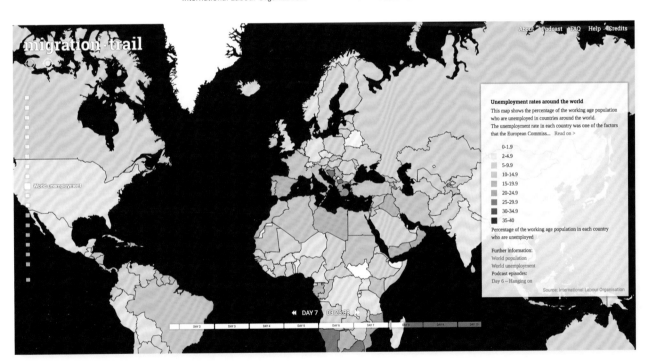

Migration trail would also not have been possible without close collaborations with colleagues from other fields, drawing a parallel with the interdisciplinary nature of traditional construction projects.

Notes
1. Wonderland, Silvia Forlati and Anne Isopp (eds), *Manual for Emerging Architects*, Springer (Vienna and New York), 2011.
2. Building Futures, *The Future for Architects?*, RIBA (London), 2011: www.buildingfutures.org.uk/assets/downloads/The_Future_for_Architects_Full_Report_2.pdf.
3. Defined by the International Organization for Migration as 'movement that takes place outside the regulatory norms of the sending, transit and receiving countries': see www.iom.int/key-migration-term

Alex Axinte and Cristi Borcan

Towards an
Intermediary Practice
Bucharest Laboratory

A major focus of studioBASAR's work is the transformation of urban spatial infrastructure through collaboration with civic groups, NGOs and public authorities. The Bucharest firm's co-founders **Alex Axinte and Cristi Borcan** here describe how lack of investment under communism, followed by a capitalist flurry of private and commercial building, left Romania's citizens short of spaces for shared activities. As illustrated by several projects, they explain how they are going about addressing this issue, through establishing tools and frameworks as well as architectural design.

Typical Bucharest neighbourhood, 2015

A characteristic socialist neighbourhood in Bucharest, of the type where more than three-quarters of the population lives: massive apartment buildings surrounded by leftover, technical and transit spaces.

Founded in 2006 in Bucharest, studioBASAR grew as an architectural studio part of the real estate bubble. Against the background of the socioeconomic crisis, the studio gradually evolved towards a public space practice, becoming both a personal and a professional vehicle for reflecting, adapting and acting within the local context. Supported both by the typical architectural practice side of the studio and by intermittent cultural funding, studioBASAR functions in survival mode, always struggling for sustainability. Long-term goals have been pursued through a collage of fragments and ad-hoc small steps, in a flexible, adaptable and opportunistic mix of approaches. Non-material contributions, such as voluntary work, have balanced out the financial precariousness while simultaneously embodying the practice's values and vision about urban living. For studioBASAR's team, its collaborators, partners and participants, this approach has produced a valuable set of non-monetary gains, from acquiring knowledge and skills, to facilitating empowerment and networking.

Distorted by a brutal dictatorship, the socialist regime undermined Romanian society's collective dimension and people's trust in the state. The drive towards individualism expanded and flourished in the public sphere after the country's 1989 revolution, and throughout the transition from socialism to capitalism, accompanied by the diminishing role of the state. The result is an increasingly divided and unequal society, where access to common resources and participation in public decision-making are shrinking, while new models of social transformation are slow to materialise.

Aiming to recover the public dimension of architectural practice, studioBASAR has initiated projects that seek to reconstruct a common ground, supporting players and practices which are constantly excluded by the dominant paradigms. By designing formats that enable collaboration between local communities, public institutions, NGOs and educational bodies, studioBASAR's latest projects articulate alternative mechanisms of co-production around transforming and managing urban spatial infrastructure.

Learning by Doing

Most of Bucharest's inhabitants live in mass housing estates. Due to the economic priorities of socialism, the inherited undersized public infrastructure of these neighbourhoods declined under the capitalist commercial narrative. Interviews and observation undertaken during studioBASAR's research projects have evidenced the neighbourhoods' lack of basic infrastructure even for meetings or social gatherings. Supermarket hallways were pointed out by the inhabitants to fill this spatial gap, acting as meeting places or venues for events – an indication of the communities' precarious public support structures. Due to its spatial resources and its presence within the community, the network of public libraries is among the few starting points for community regeneration in these neighbourhoods.

Within this context, in 2015 studioBASAR set up the City School project, which aims to reconnect the educational process to real urban actors' needs. Bucharest Metropolitan Library (BMB) became the project partner and case study for the City School's first two editions. BMB was in need of skilled partners and activation tools to support its community outreach efforts. Designed as an interdisciplinary mutual learning environment for tutors and students of architecture, sociology and landscape design, the City School engaged the participants in actions of field research, public space activation, consultation, brainstorming sessions and hands-on workshops. Financed through a corporate social responsibility (CSR) programme and involving diverse stakeholders, such as public institutions, universities and local inhabitants, the City School co-designed spatial answers tailored to the library and its nearby community's needs.

studioBASAR,
City School project second edition,
Militari neighbourhood,
Bucharest,
2017

A self-construction workshop at the Gheorghe Lazăr Library in July 2017, as part of the City School's 2016–17 edition, where the participants worked on site to produce the wooden structures for two interventions: a side alley of the nearby George Topîrceanu Library and an underused green space.

studioBASAR,
City School project first edition,
Militari neighbourhood,
Bucharest,
2016

The interior of the Gheorghe Lazăr Library transformed through a participative process and built by students during the 2015–16 edition of the City School initiative.

Going beyond its educational limitations, the project aims to build an institutional format that can scale up as a model of urban regeneration.

During the 2015–16 edition, the Gheorghe Lazăr Library reopened after years of closure at the end of a participatory process managed by tutors and students, which involved neighbours and librarians in the transformation of the library's interior. For the 2016–17 edition, the City School team went beyond the library, reclaiming for public use a side alley of the nearby George Topîrceanu Library and an underused green space in the neighbourhood, through a series of participative actions involving nearby inhabitants, neighbours' representatives and local authorities. Following inhabitants' desires and further supporting the library's active role in the community, City School's third edition is planning to transform the green space near the library. However, going beyond its educational limitations, the project aims to build an institutional format that can scale up as a model of urban regeneration.

studioBASAR,
City School project second edition,
Militari neighbourhood,
Bucharest,
2017

The 'Green Hour' planting session in May 2017, when neighbours joined City School participants in planting seeds and saplings in the green space near the George Topîrceanu Library.

The City School team in July 2017, giving the final touches to the outdoor children's library installed on the George Topîrceanu Library's exterior wall, which reclaimed a closed back alley for the neighbourhood's public use.

Spacing the New Civic Conditions

Before the 1989 revolution, the socialist state imported progressive modernist tools in the name of 'popular democracy', but used them to serve its totalitarian political vision, producing spaces of power representation and citizen exclusion, surrounded by a mass of anonymous dwellings that encouraged individual refuge. Furthermore, the subsequent capitalist period encouraged an individualistic society, which favoured enclosed, private, exclusivist and commercialised spaces. This phenomenon amounts to a planning paradigm which systematically failed to allow space for collective needs and social relations within the Romanian urban habitat.

Against this background, and as a reaction to the authorities' opacity and inability to manage common resources in the public interest, people began to react and to come together in informal civic groups. Discouraged by socialism and neglected by capitalism, the need for voluntary associations strengthened these groups in time. Supported by expertise from NGOs of community organisers like CeRe: The Resource Center for Public Participation, these groups became critical actors in Bucharest's neighbourhoods. Among them is the Lacul Tei Civic Initiative Group, with which studioBASAR has been working on place-making collaborations since 2015. Responding to a spatial need identified by the group's members, studioBASAR and the Group developed the brief and received a CSR grant to establish the Tei Community Centre. Inaugurated in October 2016, the centre is an answer to the neighbourhood's lack of local spaces for cultural dissemination, educational production and community interaction. Housed in a customised shipping container and placed in the neighbourhood's public park, it is the first community centre developed and managed by a group of citizens.

Curating its programme and planning its future activities was an experience of learning by doing for the various stakeholders involved, including citizens, NGOs, professionals and public authorities. The centre has hosted a series of events organised by the Group and by different NGOs, in line with its civic–community and cultural–educational directions. Acting as a flexible and open format, it facilitates a new set of spatial relationships among citizens, and between citizens and authorities. However, the centre's long-term challenge lies in its replication potential as a model civic institution.

An Intermediary Position

Working from within Bucharest's laboratory condition called for an interdisciplinary, experimental and innovative approach to architectural practice. This was an iterative process, based first on mapping the manifestations and protocols of the everyday, and secondly aiming to reveal the invisible mechanisms of local spatial conversations. From an intermediary position between mapping and acting, studioBASAR plays its part as an architectural practice in this conversation, not just by designing packages for the active forces of the market, but by crafting tools and creating frameworks enabling other forces to crystallise, join and make an impact. Designing spaces for learning is both a reflexive process, professionally targeted towards architecture's inner mechanisms, like education or participation, but also tailored towards the local context, which is marked by tension and distrust. Aiming to produce and disseminate success stories, studioBASAR is becoming increasingly aware of the over-evaluation of the alternative components of the practice, while the contrasting mainstream continues as usual, unchallenged. By working with public institutions and civic groups, studioBASAR's future projects are aiming to move from the margins of the professional and public discourse, towards the core mechanisms and protocols of society. ⌂

studioBASAR,
Tei Community Centre,
Circus Park,
Tei neighbourhood,
Bucharest,
2016

The inauguration of the Tei Community Centre, in a repurposed shipping container, and the opening of the photo exhibition 'Stories from Tei', organised by members of the Lacul Tei Civic Initiative Group, on 15 October 2016.

Carl Turner Architects,
Pop Brixton,
Brixton,
London,
2015

A new 'mini city' of culture,
enterprise and community on what
was previously a brownfield site
of around 2,000 square metres
(21,500 square feet), Pop Brixton,
a meanwhile-use project, has
transformed a once-derelict space
into a hive of activity, bringing
much-needed affordable work and
leisure space to the area.

THE ARCHITECT AS OPTIMIST: CARL TURNER

Becoming your own client is an obvious way of achieving autonomy and proving your full potential as an architect. Of course, that requires an understanding of finances and the property market, and an ability to calculate risk. All these are fundamental to **Carl Turner**'s practice. In conversation with Guest-Editors Chris Bryant, Caspar Rodgers and Tristan Wigfall of **alma-nac**, he describes how his first self-initiated project, for a prototype super-low-energy terraced house in South London, fed into another for a temporary community centre, and ultimately led to a major institutional commission.

From the outset Carl Turner has always had an ambition to be an architect who builds 'things'. It was while at the Royal College of Art (RCA) in London undertaking his Master's in architecture that he really fell in love with 'making stuff', taking cues from the many creative disciplines the architecture department shared the building with, most notably the furniture makers. This direct approach and willingness to get his hands dirty defined his route into practice. His first commissions as a graduate were in fact for pieces of furniture: 'We built furniture, cupboards, wardrobes, desks and eventually we built kitchens. One thing led to another and before we knew it we were building extensions to put the kitchens in.'

Turner initially formed a collaboration (Turner Castle Partnership) with fellow RCA graduate Cassion Castle in 2001, and over the subsequent five years they built an extensive body of work as architect and contractor. However, frustrations soon emerged as traditional small-practice pigeonholing meant the majority of their projects were for private residential clients. Turner's desire was to have more autonomy in his projects, and the natural way in which to achieve this was to become his own client.

Carl Turner Architects,
Home From Home,
Museu do Design e da Moda (MUDE),
Lisbon,
2011

below: The concept behind the installation was conveyed through five individual structures, each one representing a different part of the home – front room, kitchen, commode, bed and stairway – which together create a playfully abstract house and articulate ideas of British domesticity.

The temporary installation was designed, constructed and installed on site by the architects. The structures were assembled in their workshop and transported to Lisbon in a lorry, highlighting the practice's hands-on approach to the design and delivery of projects.

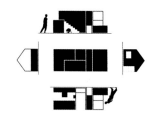
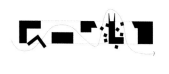

Carl Turner Architects,
Slat House,
Blackheath,
London,
2005

The practice's unusual two-storey
extension and remodelling of a
1930s semi-detached house provides
an extra bedroom, bathroom and
study/garage and opens up the
interiors during the summer.

Turner's desire was to have more autonomy in his projects, and the natural way in which to achieve this was to become his own client

Carl Turner Architects,
Stealth Barn,
Walpole St Peter,
Norfolk,
UK,
2011

A workspace and studio self-build
on the site of one of the practice's
early developments, Ochre Barn,
which involved the conversion of
a historic agricultural building into
residential accommodation. The
Stealth Barn, although delivered
within an extremely tight budget
of just £32,000, has gone on to
be one of the practice's most
published projects.

The Architect as Client/Developer

Building on the experience he gained in running a design-and-build construction firm, Turner managed to apply this skill set when embarking on his first self-initiated new-build development, the Slip House (2012), after founding London-based Carl Turner Architects in 2006. Having purchased a house in Lambeth, South London, which included a potential site to the rear, he set about designing a super-low-energy terraced house prototype that would be a model for sustainable city living. He went on to design and build the project, acting as main contractor, and remains positive about the virtues of undertaking work of this type: 'Doing your own developments is a fantastic opportunity to be unshackled, and to be able to really pursue an architectural vision without having to be so constrained by everyday concerns that might otherwise occupy a client's mind.'

The Slip House was pivotal in the evolution of his office, serving both as a training mechanism for the practice (the house was designed to the UK Code for Sustainable Homes Level 5) and ultimately providing a financial return on the sale of the property that enabled them to invest in their Pop Brixton project.

Carl Turner Architects,
Slip House,
Brixton,
London,
2012

The Slip House occupies a gap site in a typical row of terraced houses. A prototype brownfield development, it consists of three stacked boxes, pushed or slipped outwards from the back of the site towards the street. The arrangement avoids overshadowing houses to the rear and breaks up the bulk of the building.

Design, Construct and Manage

Perhaps serendipitous in nature, the origins of the Pop Brixton community project (2015) relate back to an advert in the local newspaper that Turner read while living at the Slip House. Lambeth Council launched a competition seeking ideas for potential uses for a disused plot of council-owned land that would create jobs and training, and provide affordable workspace. Critically, this was not an architectural competition, but sought ideas for both the delivery of the building and the ultimate management and running of it.

Tasked with delivering the ambitious vision that he had set out within his proposal, Turner recognised that this was something of a watershed moment for the practice. The risk-averse might have faltered at this point, but he is unashamed to admit that he is a risk taker: 'I have always taken risks. I'm not a worrier. So I don't have sleepless nights ... I can switch off. I can compartmentalise.' Investing £150,000 from the proceeds of the sale of the Slip House, he embarked on the steep learning curve of designing, constructing and managing the Pop Brixton project, a series of 60-plus shipping containers adapted to provide a temporary creative hub for community events and space for start-ups working in retail, design, food and social enterprise.

Turner is aware that the current interest in 'meanwhile' architecture may not be long lived, but he can see the longer-term benefits: 'The great thing about meanwhile projects ... is that they get us in on the conversation with landowners really early on and are leading to bigger, and not just temporary, projects.' Through another serendipitous course of events, his involvement with Pop Brixton led to the practice's transformation of a multistorey car park in Peckham, South London, into a cultural venue and arts workspace, which in turn paved the way to a commission to design the multimillion-pound Mountview Academy of Theatre Arts, also in Peckham, due for completion this year.

He went on to design and build the project, acting as main contractor, and remains positive about the virtues of undertaking projects of this type

Carl Turner Architects,
Mountview Academy of Theatre Arts,
Peckham,
London,
2018

Located on a 4,760-square-metre (51,240-square-foot) site behind the Stirling Prize-winning Peckham Library, two interlocking buildings provide both the public and private spaces required for one of the UK's leading drama schools.

Taking Risks and Pushing the Boundaries

In speaking with Turner, the overarching perception is of an architect who is willing to take risks and seek out opportunities that would not have otherwise presented themselves to him: 'The strongest projects that have come out of the office have really been my own self-initiated projects, and I think that is because we have been able to take risks and in a way be more thoughtful and conceptual, to push things to their limits.'

Turner is an accomplished designer, but also understands the wider context of property, finances and the importance of calculated risks. This has allowed him to have greater influence over projects than an architect might otherwise experience, which is evident in the quality and dynamism of his work. ᴅ

This article is based on conversations between Tristan Wigfall, Chris Bryant and Carl Turner at his London office in February 2018.

THE POWER
OF LOCALISM

Pen Sereypagna,
Mapping the White Building,
Genealogy of Bassac,
Phnom Penh,
Cambodia,
2014

Brian McGrath

Combining architectural drawings of
the White Building as built with photo
documentation of residents' adaptations,
creates a database for artists, architects,
urbanists and local people to understand
the city through a single building as a
metaphor of urban change in Cambodia.

Architectural Localism as Damage Control in the Face of Globalism and Digitisation

With everything seeming to go global and digital, how can architecture retain a healthily humanist perspective? Having identified four waves of globalisation since the 1980s, **Brian McGrath**, Professor of Urban Design at New York's Parsons School of Design, explores how architects from the US to Southeast Asia have recently been addressing their various challenges by evolving a new localism – whether through acknowledging typomorphological rules of place, using portable architecture to lighten impact, supporting creative local entrepreneurship, or taking a political stance.

The postcolonial literary theorist Gayatri Spivak has written that globalisation takes place only in the immaterial realms of data and capital. Everything else – the humanities, aesthetics and even daily life – is relegated to damage control.[1] While architectural ideas and construction products circulate around the globe, building is always local, and remains the most material form of resistance to globalisation. Born at the tail end of the baby boom, my generation witnessed the social revolutions of the 1960s as children rather than participants. We began professional practice in architecture during the 1980s, with the radical ideals of our immediate seniors in our heads, but the reality of a new world order around us. Our professional coming of age coincided with the beginning of the neoliberal, revanchist counter-revolution that replaced progressive secular socialism with a return of religious fundamentalism and market capitalism.[2] As witnesses to this shift, we became translators of the ideals of the 1960s to the next generation of architects who carried on the project of local resistance to the social and environmental damage that results from digital and financial globalisation.

The story of architectural localism can be articulated as a resistance to four waves of globalisation: (1) the unfolding of the digital globalisation of finance capital in the 1980s; (2) the emergence of the World Wide Web and digital architectural software in the 1990s; (3) the invention of text messaging, the smartphone and massive data collection in the 2000s; and (4) the tsunami of social media fuelling the Occupy movement in the 2010s. Each decade has had its own battles to maintain a social commitment to the power of architectural localism as 'damage control' in the face of such transformations in everyday life.

Green Guerillas,
Community garden,
East Village,
New York City,
1986

In the 1980s, community gardens proliferated in vacant lots in New York City's East Village in the shadow of a reinvigorated Wall Street. Originally the idea of the Green Guerillas, the city later adopted the Green Thumb programme that rented the land to community gardeners for $1 per year.

Located

Following the conversion of the New York Stock Exchange from paper to electronic trading in the 1980s, New York City began to emerge from a long period of population and economic decline. The neighbourhoods of Lower Manhattan became disrupted by the sudden increase in real-estate values, especially in the artists' districts that mixed with leftover industries in Tribeca and Soho, Jane Jacobs's sleepy Greenwich Village, and the immigrant melting pot of the Lower East Side. While Jacobs's articulation of the value and attributes of a socially mixed urban neighbourhood of small streets and blocks, and the transformation of Soho into an artists' district for a short period of time, are well documented, there were several less well-known experiments in radical neighbourhood localism, inspired by feminist and environmentalist movements, among the abandoned tenements and vacant lots across town in the East Village. Examples include the Cooper Square Committee founded by Emma Goldman and Thelma Burdick, Liz Christy's Green Guerillas, and Ellen Stewart's La MaMa experimental theatre, which became the basis of Fourth Street Arts Block. While the rural village may have represented the ideal of a pastoral localism in a previous time, the vibrant bottom-up regeneration of urban neighbourhoods has become the battleground of localism at the turn of the 21st century.

Though written in Italian in the 1960s, the new English translation of Aldo Rossi's book *The Architecture of the City* in 1982 provided the basis for US architects to reinvest in the ancient Roman concept of 'locus'.[3] Rossi advocated the careful historical study of urban neighbourhoods as a set of typological rules and morphological responses to the specifics of place, site, climate, geography and history. For him, the city was the locus of a society's collective memory, and the field of architecture provided the best disciplinary lens through which to 'read' these socially constructed typomorphological rules of a place. While Rossi considered himself neither modern nor postmodern, the first Venice Architecture Biennale, established in 1980 with the 'Strada Novissima' exhibition, ushered in an era of architecture catching the wave of the new neoliberal economy and the spectacle of global media. Architecture as spectacle in the 1980s directly competed with Rossi's more radical theories of the 1960s. The architecture of the city formed the basis of a rational and structural approach to the social and environmental activism of earlier decades.

While Manhattan and Brooklyn benefited immediately from the new fortunes of Wall Street, more distant immigrant neighbourhoods continued to decline in this immaterial economy of finance and real-estate speculation. Madeline Ruiz and Dave Robinson located themselves in the working-class Ironbound neighbourhood of Newark, New Jersey, shortly after graduation in 1991 and founded the Studio for Urban Architecture and Design (SUAD) in 2004, establishing a professional portfolio focused on adaptive reuse of the area's post-industrial landscape. One of their first projects was FIXbruen (2010), the addition of three floors atop a converted single-storey garage. The mixed-use building includes a ground-floor office, a one-bedroom loft flat as well as a duplex apartment with a spacious roof deck. Outdoor oases in an urban setting are also essential to the practice. In parallel, they took on the legacy of corrupt local governance by challenging the proliferation of commuter parking lots, promoting sensible planning, supporting the local Ironbound Community Corporation, and advocating for parks, playgrounds and open spaces such as the new Lafayette Street School Playground for the neighbourhood primary school, which was completed this year with the support of the Trust for Public Land.

SUAD's conception was developed with innovative adaptations of the buildings and textures of a working-class, immigrant neighbourhood in a post-industrial city. Sensitive integration of local artistic treatments is the trademark of the firm, and their ongoing collaboration with clients, artisans and craftspeople gives each of their projects extraordinary individualism, marked with a depth of texture, light and form. Custom-designed furniture and interior architectural elements are also of importance in their design approach. SUAD works closely with expert craftspeople to manufacture these pieces. Seating, lighting, floor and ceiling applications are often the custom product of the seamless collaboration between architect and artisan.

Studio of Urban Architecture (SUAD),
FIXbruen,
Ironbound,
Newark,
New Jersey,
2010

SUAD salvaged all of the beams and added two-and-a-half floors to a former single-storey garage, creating a mixed-use home-work loft building with the original ground floor devoted to a professional office.

The Trust for Public Land,
Lafayette Street School Playground,
Newark,
New Jersey,
2018

Through tireless advocacy, SUAD spearheaded the transformation of a parking lot used by schoolteachers into a playground in partnership with the Trust for Public Land, Newark Public Schools and the Lafayette Street School community.

all(zone),
SZL market,
Bangkok,
2012

SZL shelters both the popular localism of traditional open-air markets, while also accommodating franchise mini-marts for the new suburban middle-class.

Light House, featured at the 2015 Chicago Architecture Biennial, is a nomadic micro-dwelling prototype for minimal, low-cost living in tropical megacities that can be erected within abandoned towers.

all(zone),
Light House,
Chicago Architecture Biennial,
2015

The art of living lightly. Highly portable, Light House can be dismantled, moved in a package slightly larger than a suitcase, and easily reassembled to temporarily occupy vacancies in high-priced cities.

Dislocated

In *Modernity at Large* (1996), anthropologist and globalisation theorist Arjun Appadurai redefines the 'production of locality' in a globalising world.[4] His views of locality as relational and contextual rather than scalar or spatial turned out to be highly prophetic given the social immediacy offered by new technologies of interactivity. For Appadurai, traditional place-based locality has been sharply altered by global media yet it is within physical neighbourhoods where locality is still situated and realised. If in traditional societies the production of locality was a constant effort to counter the forces of nature and entropy, in contemporary urban life it struggles against national regimes, mass mediation and commodification.

If globalisation of financial capital was achieved through the digitalisation of stock markets, architecture schools in the US attracted a more global student population with the early introduction of digital technology, such as the Paperless Studio at Columbia University, New York, in the 1990s. Rachaporn Choochuey graduated from Columbia in 1998 and received her PhD from Tokyo University in 2002. She returned back to her home in Bangkok to establish the studio all(zone) in 2009. As its parenthetical name implies, the studio brings together collaborators from across disciplinary and national borders to produce a new kind of contemporary localism based in the ever-changing tropical megacity. As the website proclaims, they 'create alternative built environments where all could feel "at home" in the world'.[6] Like SUAD, all(zone) established a practice of architectural localism with the construction of a home/studio in the shop-house neighbourhood context of postwar expansion Bangkok (2009), but their work is an example of a 'portable' localism that we carry around the world.

The interpretation of a portable locality of the everyday is critical of the spectacular globalisation tied to data and capital. Many of all(zone)'s projects take on Appadurai's challenge of architectural localism resisting the normative understanding of place and tradition by practising what they call 'the art of living lightly'. SZL market (2012) is a light metal-frame structure, the tent-like form of which allows the fluctuation of events and encourages the plasticity of space, which is perhaps its genius loci. Light House, featured at the 2015 Chicago Architecture Biennial, is a nomadic micro-dwelling prototype for minimal, low-cost living in tropical megacities that can be erected within abandoned towers.

Relocated

As Spivak has written, globalisation takes place in the realm of data as well as capital. Digital forms of architectural practice have invited new transdisciplinary collaborations as well as transnational forms of architectural localism. Funded by the National Science Foundation, since 1997 the Baltimore Ecosystem Study (BES) has operated within a multiscalar notion of ecological localism that ties natural processes at the regional scale to social reproduction in urban neighbourhoods in and around the city. It advocates social-ecological approaches to local damage control in areas of urban disinvestment and environmental degradation. Appadurai defines locality as something that needs work to maintain human settlements against all kinds of dangers and risks. Traditionally, the production of locality ritualises anxieties of impermanence, but also gives value, meaning and legibility to natural resource limitations and environmental risks. BES's production of a social-ecological locality requires regular hard community-based work under conditions of anxiety and entropy, social injustice, ecological uncertainty and cosmic volatility.[6]

Phanat Xanamane has furthered the conceptual human ecosystem and patch dynamics frameworks he learned as a member of the BES urban design working group in New York through the establishment of Envision da Berry (EdB), a non-profit organisation in Iberia Parish, Louisiana, that he founded with Amelia Cronan in 2011.[7] Xanamane was born in Thailand, in a Laotian refugee camp, during the Vietnam War. A product of 'dislocalism', he grew up and moved to Iberia Parish, thriving under the entrepreneurial spirit of the Laotian diaspora in the American South. Incorporating his educational and professional experience with the BES, which included a stint with noted artist Mary Miss, EdB's aim is to strengthen the local economy by promoting small business development through youth-oriented creative entrepreneurship.

Envision da Berry (EdB),
da Berry Fresh,
New Iberia,
Louisiana,
2017

The project provides new jobs, community-supported agriculture, affordable healthy produce and job training.

Envision da Berry (EdB),
George Washington Carver Community Garden,
New Iberia,
Louisiana,
2016

EdB worked with the Housing Authority of New Iberia by leading efforts in procuring the startup funds as well as orchestrating the volunteer efforts to get the garden designed, built and ready for planting.

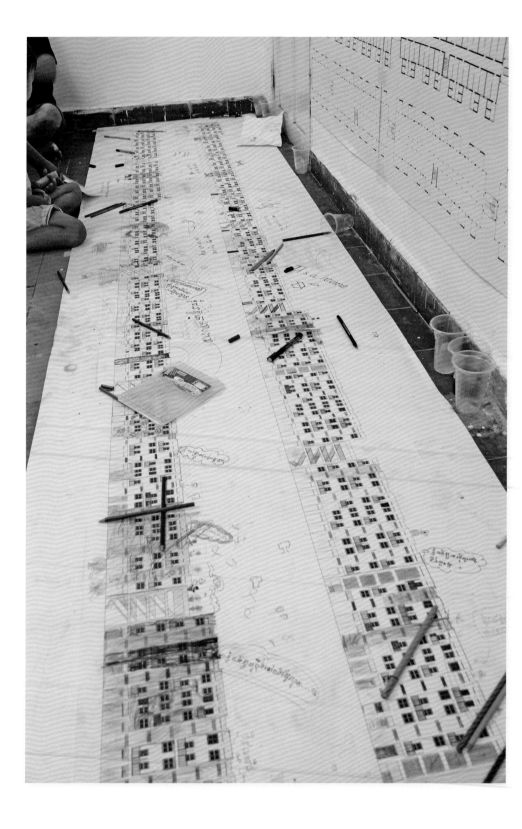

Pen Sereypagna,
Community mapping exercise,
Genealogy of Bassac,
Phnom Penh,
Cambodia,
2016

The project also engaged with the White
Building community by encouraging them
to participate in creating a new dialogue
to serve as a basis for ideas about the
future of the city.

The future of such practices in architectural
localism will continue to be challenged in
a world that will soon integrate artificial
intelligence and robotic production.

Starting with an ambitious masterplan for the da Berry neighbourhood, EdB has already built a combination of fresh produce market and job training programme (da Berry Fresh), as well as the George Washington Carver Community Garden at public housing complex AB Simon Homes, and has hosted multiple public art festivals and community planning events. The organisation has successfully reframed an area in decline as part of a vibrant tourist economy with cultural, culinary and historical significance. An important part of the success has been a performance, entertainment and social media campaign. As an openly gay Asian refugee, Xanamane has led an organisation that has broken down the many racial and social barriers to provide a counter-localism for the future of the American South.

Occupy

The second decade of the 21st century began with the occupation of Wall Street in 2011, first in front of the New York Stock Exchange, then a more long-term takeover of Zuccotti Park. The Occupy Wall Street movement began as an online social media campaign, but marked the beginning of the assertion of politically active architectural localism that has flourished ever since. Cambodian architect Pen Sereypagna entered the architectural profession in this current decade with Genealogy of Bassac (2014–), a research study that focuses on an informal neighbourhood that occupied a cultural waterfront district built during the 1960s, and in particular the 300-metre (1,000-foot) long White Building, a Modernist housing slab that became home to artists and performers following the end of the Khmer Rouge in 1979.[8]

Genealogy of Bassac explores both Cambodian Prime Minister Hun Sen's new globalising casino urbanism in Phnom Penh and the establishment of a counter-localism in places like the White Building, constructed by a new creative generation who have come of age without any direct memory of the Khmer Rouge. Pen's study of the White Building, and the Bassac neighbourhood that surrounds it is a community-based, participatory mapping of the residents, artists and architects who have grown up there through five decades of exile, return and eviction. A key objective was to discover ways to visualise the characteristics of societal ruptures through various historical eras as reflected in the details of daily life in this particular locality.

The genealogy presents an urban palimpsest consisting of both visible and invisible layers that records the memory of triumph and sorrow, boom and bust, the heroic and the mundane. The project layers as forms of knowledge the tactics of architectural localism for a community experiencing a rapid transformation. The genealogical methodology looks at both descent and emergence – backwards and forward – throughout Phnom Penh's complex history, as inheritor of the Khmer Empire, satellite city of French colonial Indochina, the site of early cosmopolitan independent cultural experiments in architecture and urban planning, and of exodus during the Khmer Rouge regime. Bassac is a locality of memory; its future is happening now, with the displacement of the massive informal reoccupation of the city and its rise as a new node in the global neoliberal economy.

Global Localism

Borrowing from Spivak, this article has introduced the idea that architectural localism has been a humanist 'damage control' response to the globalisation of data and capital. Each decade has witnessed the introduction of new strategies and technologies to rapidly distribute capital and scientific data across the globe, which have been countered by new tactics of architectural localism. For SUAD, an immigrant urban neighbourhood became the locus of carefully crafted projects that were a continuum of the collective memory of a post-industrial city in the wake of the digitalisation and globalisation of finance. An early modern shop-house neighbourhood in Bangkok has become the hub for all(zone) to experiment with the art of living lightly, a portable localism in a decade where internet communication connected architecture practices around the world. Envision da Berry has transformed a declining neighbourhood into an invigorated cultural hub at a time of ubiquitous social media. And a Genealogy of Bassac represents a new generation of artists, architects and activists in Phnom Penh who are challenging rapid urban development by valorising the early modern architecture and planning in Cambodia as well as the rights of people to occupy the city. The future of such practices in architectural localism will continue to be challenged in a world that will soon integrate artificial intelligence and robotic production. Architecture will only grow in importance, not in catching the latest wave of the globalisation of data and capital, but in creating environments for making a place that is socially equitable and ecologically sustainable. ⌂

Notes
1. Gayatri Spivak, *An Aesthetic Education in the Age of Globalization*, Harvard University Press (Cambridge, MA), 2012.
2. Christian Caryl, *Strange Rebels: 1979 and the Birth of the 21st Century*, Basic Books (New York), 2014.
3. Aldo Rossi, *The Architecture of the City*, MIT Press (Cambridge, MA), 1982.
4. Arjun Appadurai, *Modernity at Large: Cultural Dimensions of Globalization*, University of Minnesota Press (Minnesota, MN), 1996.
5. www.allzonedesignall.com/who-we-are/.
6. Appadurai, *op cit*.
7. www.daberry.org/.
8. https://genealogyofbassac.wordpress.com/.

Co-produced Urban Resilience

A Framework for Bottom-Up Regeneration

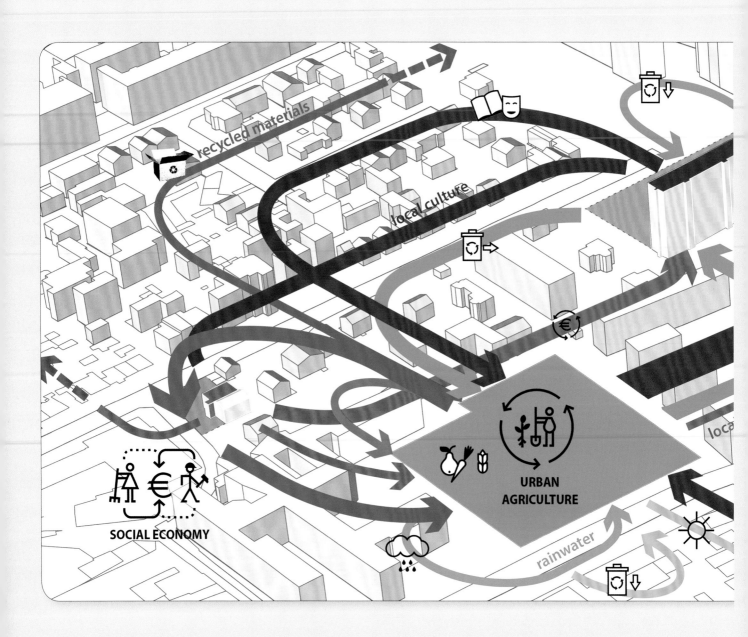

recycled materials

local culture

URBAN AGRICULTURE

SOCIAL ECONOMY

rainwater

loca

atelier d'architecture autogérée (aaa),
R—Urban ecological principles,
2011

Constantin Petcou
and Doina Petrescu

Where the welfare state has failed, can a new civic economy succeed? **Constantin Petcou and Doina Petrescu** co-founded atelier d'architecture autogérée to explore participatory urbanism as an answer to today's environmental and economic challenges. One result is R-Urban, a framework centred around 'civic hubs' that allows communities to enhance their resilience through a range of interconnected initiatives. Implemented in neighbourhoods in the Paris area and London, it can be adapted to any location and scaled up to have an impact on a regional level and beyond.

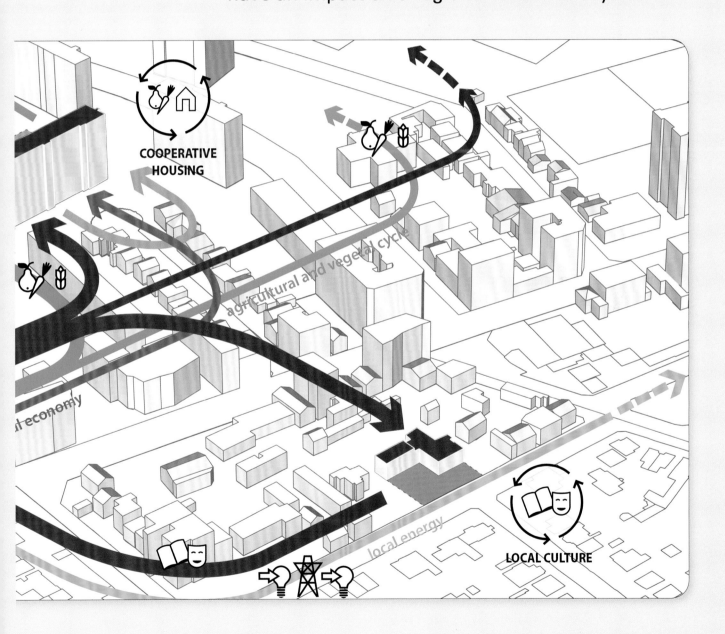

COOPERATIVE HOUSING

agricultural and vegetal cycle

local economy

local energy

LOCAL CULTURE

The R-Urban civic hubs function through locally closed circuits, balancing consumption and production, reducing CO2 emissions and encouraging people to live and work more ecologically. Water, compost and waste can be collected and treated locally, so that food can also be produced locally rather than travelling long distances.

'Co-production' has become a buzzword in these times of crisis and austerity, positing the necessity to engage citizens collectively in self-provision in a context in which the welfare state is no longer there to organise public services. In the context of city transformation, it can also be understood as a political project rooted in the idea of a 'social production of space' developed by the French sociologist Henri Lefebvre in the 1970s.[1] Under the current imperative to adapt and find solutions to the long-term environmental and economic crises societies face today, our cities need to become more resilient. And this need to be able to adjust and thrive in rapidly changing circumstances, which cities have little capacity to deal with at this moment in time, comes with a right to resilience for all citizens – a right to be informed about, decide, act upon and manage the future of their urban environments.

Claiming the right to resilience for all is an ambitious co-production project that should involve the entire urban population. It needs ideas, tools and spaces, time and agency, and therefore agents and activators. Can architects be such agents? What tools and means can be used in times of crisis and scarcity? How can progressive practices be initiated while acting locally and on a small scale? How can civic cultures of collaboration and sharing be reactivated and sustained in economic, environmental and social terms alike?

R-Urban Principles

R-Urban, a framework for bottom-up resilient urban regeneration initiated by atelier d'architecture autogérée (aaa) in 2008, is one of the many small-scale initiatives to have emerged in response to the slow pace of governmental procedures and lack of consensus in further addressing the challenges of global crisis and evaluating their consequences for people's lives. Conceived as an open-source strategy that can adapt to any local context, it enables residents to play an active part in changing the city while also changing their ways of living in it. Already implemented in towns in the Paris region and London, it creates a network of citizen projects and grassroots organisations around a series of self-managed collective facilities. These 'civic hubs' host economic, ecological and cultural activities and everyday practices such as food growing, cooking, beekeeping, repairing, recycling, compost making and community energy production that contribute to boosting resilience in an urban context.

The hubs are openly programmed depending on local social and economic assets. The network acts through locally closed circuits that activate material (water, energy, waste and food) and immaterial (know-how and culture) flows between key fields of activity (economy, habitation and urban agriculture) that are already in place or could be implemented within the existing city fabric. It begins at neighbourhood level and progressively scales to

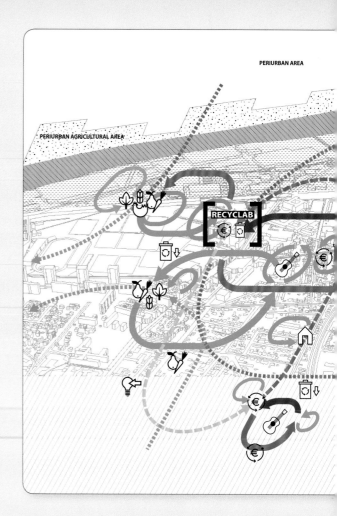

atelier d'architecture autogérée (aaa),
R-Urban implementation,
Colombes, Paris, 2011

The first R-Urban network emerges around three collective hubs – Agrocité, Recyclab and Ecohab – in the suburban town of Colombes.

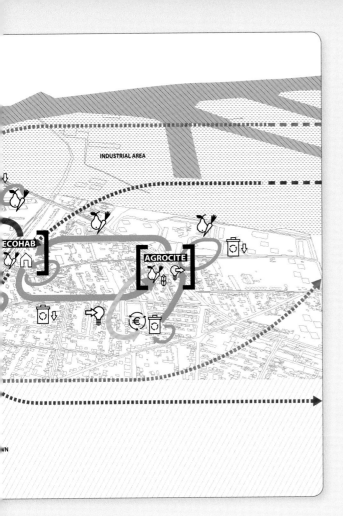

INDUSTRIAL AREA

ECOHAB

AGROCITE

These first
implementations
were intended to
test the adaptability
and replicability
of the model in
different contexts,
with the aim of
advocating for
new policies and
funding streams
to support further
developments.

the city and regional levels, resulting in small-scale impacts that create larger-scale outputs.

Although it has been conceived and initiated by architectural designers, R-Urban's specificity is that the framework itself is co-produced and open to a diverse range of actors. It addresses communities from urban and suburban contexts, and engages residents, local authorities, public organisations, professionals and civic stakeholders to take various responsibilities in its governance. In contrast to other regeneration proposals conceived by specialist teams and facilitated by managerial structures, the designers, architects and planners here take an active role as initiators, facilitators, mediators and consultants in civic partnerships. This leads to a more effective, faster and more sustainable implementation, and allows for greater participation of non-specialists in co-producing it.

R-Urban begins by identifying the need to connect local resilience initiatives in order to increase their agency and impact, and then building support and partnerships for funding and implementation. This approach has been enabled by the nature of aaa's practice, which is both an interdisciplinary professional structure and a non-governmental organisation. This status has enabled the studio to be civic and professional at the same time, to garner support for its social work and to be able to conduct high-standing professional and research projects. Its funders are mainly public bodies (EU, national, regional and municipal governments and research agencies). It sustains itself through 'diverse economies', to borrow JK Gibson-Graham's term,[2] including project-based research and cultural funding, academic wages, professional commissions, voluntary and activist work, all of which are considered equally important, and necessary for the nature of its work as a research-based activist–professional practice.

Urban Resilience Hubs
The first implementation of R-Urban was in Colombes, a suburban town of 84,000 inhabitants near Paris. The strategy was presented to the local council, with whom aaa then set up a partnership that also included a number of civic organisations and local residents, and Public Works, a critical design practice that occupies the terrain in-between architecture, art, performance and activism, working in Hackney Wick in London. These first implementations were intended to test the adaptability and replicability of the model in different contexts, with the aim of advocating for new policies and funding streams to support further developments.

As part of an environmental innovation project funded by the EU, in 2013/14 three R-Urban hubs were planned in Colombes of which only two were built (Agrocité and Recyclab). A further hub was built in London (R-Urban Wick). Collectively run, their architecture showcases the various issues they address, such as local materials recycling, local skills, energy production and food growing.

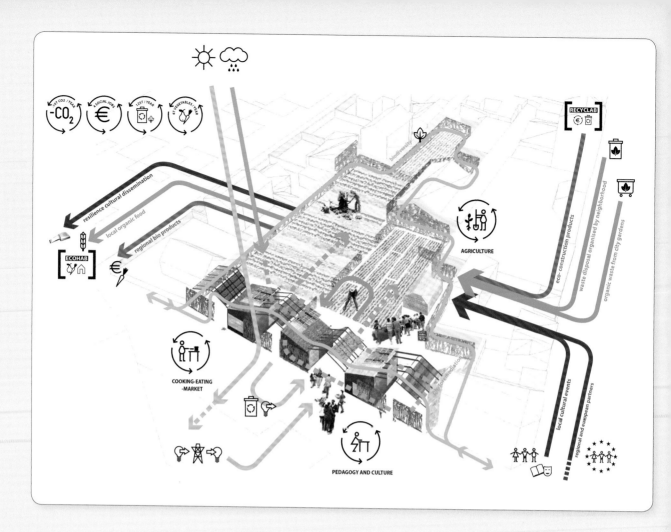

RECYCLAB

resilience cultural dissemination

local organic food

regional bio products

ECOHAB

AGRICULTURE

eco-construction products

waste disposal organised by neighborhood

organic waste from city gardens

COOKING-EATING
-MARKET

PEDAGOGY AND CULTURE

local cultural events

regional and european partners

atelier d'architecture autogérée (aaa),
Agrocité, Colombes, Paris, 2013

above: The Agrocité hub consists of an experimental micro-farm, collective gardens, education and cultural facilities, a community cafe and local mini-market. The project was conceived to include ecological closed circuits: electricity is produced on site, rainwater is collected and greywater is phyto-filtered to be used for crops, and compost is made on site.

above: Agrocité transforms a temporarily available derelict plot into a space for agricultural and civic co-production.

right: An aerial view of the neighbourhood shows a productive landscape maintained by the inhabitants of the social housing estate who can see the results of their collective endeavour from their balconies.

Recycled components are used for cladding and floor surfaces.

Agrocité is an agricultural unit comprising an experimental micro-farm, community gardens, pedagogical and cultural spaces, as well as a series of experimental devices for compost heating, rainwater collection for garden irrigation, solar energy production, and greywater phyto-remediation. It is a hybrid structure, whereby some components are run as social enterprises (the micro-farm, market, worm compost farm and cafe) and others by local organisations (community garden, teaching and cultural spaces).

Recyclab functions as a social enterprise. A recycling and eco-construction unit, it has several facilities for storing and reusing locally salvaged materials, recycling and transforming them into elements for self-building and retrofitting. An associated 'fab lab' for local residents has also been set up.

Both hubs were originally located on temporarily available public land and are reversible building designs, meaning they can easily be relocated in time. This reversibility is an ecological principle implying that the site can be reinvested by other urban programmes according to evolving needs and conditions, and that the building itself can be dismantled, rebuilt using most of its original materials and infrastructures, and repurposed in another context for different users.

atelier d'architecture autogérée (aaa),
Recyclab, Colombes, Paris, 2014

Cargo bike prototypes realised at Recyclab, a recycling and eco-construction hub that hosts community makers' workshops and design studios.

Network Expansion and Development

As such, in 2018 the Agrocité and Recyclab hubs were relocated and rebuilt in the Parisian communes of Gennevilliers and Nanterre, and a new hub was constructed in Bagneux. The R-Urban network is planned to grow in the next few years and to be managed by a Cooperative Land Trust that will acquire space, facilitate development and guarantee democratic governance. Current stakeholders include existing local and professional organisations, and institutions at the regional and national level, as well as social entrepreneurs and ordinary citizens.

In addition to encouraging citizens to take active roles, the framework allows them to acquire the necessary skills and creates opportunities for them to invent their own jobs as part of a new economy. This alternative economy is not only financial, but also, crucially, social, cognitive and affective. Individual members are signatories of the R-Urban Charter and part of the Cooperative Land Trust; however, there are also larger units that provide specific resources for the whole network, such as training and financial support. One such example is the Wiki Village Factory (WVF), a social and environmental innovation cluster that was conceived as a kind of headquarters for the R-Urban network. Currently under construction and due for completion in 2020, the 7,500-square-metre (80,730-square-foot) building in Paris's 20th arrondissement acts as an innovation platform and a place for meeting, gathering and sharing between progressive professionals and active citizens in the areas of circular economy and ecological transition. The WVF is owned by a collective real-estate company involving two social investors, and co-managed by a users' collective.

atelier d'architecture autogérée (aaa),
Wiki Village Factory (WVF),
Paris,
due for completion 2020

above: An ecological circuits diagram shows the principles that informed the design and environmental co-management of the Wiki Village Factory building.

right: In its second-prize entry for the Reinventing Paris competition, aaa proposed a 7,500-square-metre (80,730-square-foot) cluster of social and ecological innovation located in a square near Place d'Italie that was conceived as a headquarters for the R-Urban network. The project is currently under construction on a different site in the 20th arrondissement.

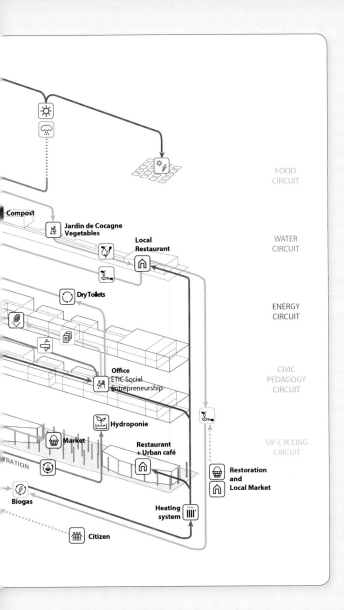

FOOD
CIRCUIT

Compost

Jardin de Cocagne
Vegetables

Local
Restaurant

WATER
CIRCUIT

Dry Toilets

ENERGY
CIRCUIT

Office
ETIC Social
Entrepreneurship

CIVIC
PEDAGOGY
CIRCUIT

Hydroponie

Market

Restaurant
+ Urban café

UP-CYCLING
CIRCUIT

Restoration
and
Local Market

Biogas

Heating
system

Citizen

This transformation needs to take place at the micro scale of each individual, each subjectivity, to build a culture of co-produced resilience at the macro scale.

Co-produced Resilience at the Macro Scale

The ambition of R-Urban is not only to investigate aspects of sustainability and resilience by means of practice, but also to practically explore societal change and political and cultural reinvention. A city region can only become resilient with the active involvement of its diverse inhabitants. To enhance democratic engagement of citizens and other stakeholders, we need new tools, knowledge and sites for testing various initiatives. We also need to establish new collective practices and to showcase the results and benefits of a resilient transformation of the city. And this is where architects have an important role to play. Rather than acting merely as building designers, architects can be initiators, negotiators, co-managers and enablers of processes and agencies that strengthen existing and emerging proposals for civic resilience. Local governments also need to play a new role in such citizen initiatives, by allowing new types of civic self-managed facilities to transpire and persist. In this passage from the welfare state to a civic economy, new forms of public–civic partnerships should be key components.

Unlike other initiatives that deal with sustainability from an exclusively technological and environmental perspective, R-Urban advocates a specific cultural and political change in terms of how we do things in order to shape our future. It constructs new collective practices of civic resilience that both reduce the ecological footprint and contribute to reinventing relationships between individuals and collectives. This transformation needs to take place at the micro scale of each individual, each subjectivity, to build a culture of co-produced resilience at the macro scale. It requires processes of reskilling, skill sharing, social networking and mutual learning, the appropriate locus for which is provided by the R-Urban framework: a networked infrastructure managed by the citizens themselves that enhances local capacity to invent and transform by proposing concrete ways of bypassing current barriers. ᗡ

Notes
1. Henri Lefebvre, *The Production of Space,* Blackwell (New York), 1991. First published 1974.
2. JK Gibson-Graham, 'Diverse Economies: Performative Practices for "Other Worlds"', *Progress in Human Geography*, 32 (5), 2008, pp 613–63.

Lys Villalba Rubio, Juan Chacón Gragera
and Manuel Domínguez Fernández

Collective Intelligences
The Future is Hybrid

Zoohaus,
Inteligencias Colectivas,
Akoo prototype,
Malabo,
Equatorial Guinea,
2013

This self-managed multipurpose
installation, built in collaboration with
Malabo's Centro Cultural de España
(Spanish cultural centre) and in its
courtyard, recovers and hybridises
local know-how lost during the oil era,
such as nipa plaiting, and evolves it
with new techniques and materials to
address contemporary needs.

Smart construction is not limited to modern technological innovation. Generations of people across the globe have evolved countless ingenious solutions to their particular needs that it would be foolish to sweep aside in the pursuit of progress. Inteligencias Colectivas is a research project run by Madrid-based Zoohaus Collective which works with communities to produce locally relevant urban prototypes that blend traditional and high-tech knowhow and materials. Zoohaus co-founders **Lys Villalba Rubio, Juan Chacón Gragera and Manuel Domínguez Fernández** introduce some examples of their projects in Africa, Asia and South America.

Every region of the world has its own repertoire of construction techniques. Although perfectly adapted to environmental conditions and shaped by their social and technological realms, these repertoires are gradually disappearing and being discarded under a globalised standardisation of processes and conception of progress.

Tacit citizenship agreements, self-made devices and half-breed techniques are pure open-code knowledge, taught by imitation and improved through years of trial-and-error experimentation. While these manifestations of human creativity are not considered valuable in professional contexts, they offer an endless source of inspiration and learning that should be considered as an asset to architects, urban planners and designers in order to improve perspectives on cities' future development.

Inteligencias Colectivas (IC) is an ongoing research and construction initiative founded in 2010 by the networking platform Zoohaus Collective, which itself was established in Madrid in 2007 to address critical and emergent concerns on urban environments. A non-profit organisation, Zoohaus was formed by young Spanish architects working in parallel to their different studios. The association is economically self-sustained with a remuneration for the members and collaborators involved in every new project. Every new endeavour, whether commissioned or self-generated, is managed differently and is funded by grants or by public and private initiatives hiring Zoohaus services. The IC team's approach is quite unlike the traditional conception of cooperation.

An open tool for design and research, IC brings together real-life examples of smart constructions and hybridises them with contemporary needs through cutting-edge prototypes. Its theoretical-practical methodology consists of bidirectional teaching–learning processes, taking feedback and organising urban actions hand in hand with local collaborators, delivering unexpected solutions – with the certainty that true urban innovation comes from agreements between apparently unlikely partners. It also works as a design, architecture and urban examples database. Since 2010 more than 20 on-site workshops in 15 different countries have been developed that have categorised and created a taxonomy of intelligent urban solutions, uploading and sharing them under Creative Commons licences. All this information comes together in an online database in five sections: the 'Catalog' section is a compendium of local collective know-how discovered all over the world; 'Upgrade' is a technically drawn compilation that details features and mechanisms; 'Prototyping' consists of critical architectural elements from an assortment of solutions developed by IC members in collaboration with local communities, experts and institutions through building workshops; 'Human network' is an active knowledge network of citizen-experts; and these first four categories are geolocalised in last section, the Map.

To broaden the IC project, five locations around the world – Manila (Philippines), Karachi (Pakistan), Malabo (Equatorial Guinea), Lagos (Nigeria) and the small Caribbean village of Palomino in Colombia – have been selected to teach us how to redefine the logics of the architecture and urbanism profession and evolve urban planning paradigms that are still firmly attached to 20th-century ideals.

Zoohaus,
Inteligencias
Colectivas,
Kalamansi
prototype,
'Rolling Manila'
project, Manila,
Philippines,
2017

Food stall prototyping workshop using pedicab and jeepney production technologies and their capacity for upgrading. Inteligencias Colectivas's (IC's) proposal – in collaboration with the Spanish Embassy of Manila, Design Center of the Philippines, Intramuros Administration and Escuela Taller – involves production of 100 stalls at separate locations all over the city.

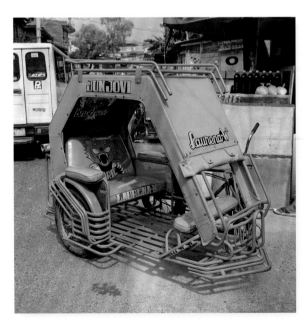

Pedicab,
Manila,
Philippines,
2017

Among Manila's many types of wheeled devices, pedicabs are the most popular. These smart means of transport are totally custom-made on the sidewalks, using only one material: 20-millimetre (¾-inch) hollow iron tubes, and handmade bending tools specifically invented to produce them.

Technological Transfers: Manila

Manila is a city on wheels. Through the decades, a whole heterogeneous family of moving devices has gradually come into being to attend to a 24/7 flow of 20 million inhabitants constantly commuting and snacking. The first specific local wheeled species to appear was the jeepney, a collective transportation model based on the technical and aesthetic customisation of thousands of old military Jeeps that the American army abandoned when they left the country after the Second World War. As if in a Darwinian dream, the wheeled family continued to evolve. New members such as 'owners' (small jeepneys), tricycles, wheeled food stalls and 'kuligligs' became a part of this self-built ecosystem, the most famous of which is the sheltered-sidecar bicycle-taxi known as the pedicab, a prolific device that has changed the face of Manila using just one material and one technique: the bending of 20-millimetre (¾-inch) hollow iron tubes. The fact that pedicabs are totally handmade and flexible enough to meet any personal style or future upgrades makes their design unbeatable. Enhanced by tropical weather and the animated street life that characterises Filipino culture, Manila's sidewalks became a distributed factory for these citizens-on-wheels.

International corporations are now starting to take on this wheeled panorama, trying to absorb the design and production of these vending and transportation elements. Obviously their assembly-line logics will not consider vendors' needs, nor local climate conditions, materials or unexpected uses. To address this technological conflict, could lessons be learned from pedicabs and jeepneys by transferring the intelligence they represent into an architectural device? Could self-organised, distributed production and customisation expertise be incorporated into legal and safe architectural processes? For two weeks of November 2017, architects, street vendors, designers, welders, students and government employees worked together to deliver the Kalamansi prototype, an upgraded version of a typical food stall that grasps these questions by testing a technological transfer from wheeled Manila to snacking Manila.

Distributed Knowledge: Karachi

The megacity of Karachi, home to a population estimated at 25 million, produces everything it needs through a network of specialised communities. Inside the rectangular urban grid, planned at the time of the British colony and now covered with a perennial layer of dust, the outdated facades hide a vast network of expert citizens arranged in productive hubs that form a true city of makers. These 'guilds', organised into 'markets' or neighbourhoods, are able to manage, process and manufacture every existing material (paper, cloth, wood, metal, truck and trolley parts etc) and through informal, unregistered associations they will build anything you can imagine, from the smallest object to the biggest city infrastructure. Each 'market' works as a self-contained unit yet is interconnected, almost synaptically, with the rest to exchange or collaborate in whatever way is needed. Everything can be done in the streets of Karachi; the city lives by the motto: 'Why import anything if we can build it here?'

This IC project enrolled part of this enormous human network as collaborators to understand and share their techniques as well as facts about local culture. These people from a wide variety of backgrounds (builders, artisans, artists, city planners, negotiators etc) came together for some weeks in November 2016 to design and build the Jugaad installation – a playful urban element on Pakistan Chowk, the public square at the heart of the city. It illustrates how environments can be configured to create distributed projects and decision-making. Only by introducing the maximum number of agents, knowledge and expertise can equitable tools be designed for the complexity and diversity that real-life cities contain.

Truck tuning, Karachi, Pakistan, 2016

For the construction of the Jugaad prototype, the IC team collaborated with the labour union responsible for the conversion of Pakistani local trucks into mobile 'fantasies'. These 'truck artists', as they call themselves, are able to dismantle, soup up and rebuild a truck within a few days.

Evolving Local Expertise for Contemporary Needs: Malabo

At some point after discovering oil stocks in the mid-1990s, Equatorial Guinea forgot how to generate what it consumes. The productive apparatus of this small isolated country gradually stopped. Nowadays everything is imported; their everyday vegetables are grown in Cameroon, their construction materials are made in China. Even their traditional textiles with exuberant patterns have to make an 8,000-kilometre (5,000-mile) trip from India to reach the shelves at the street-market tailor shops. It seems as if every single Guinean object is made elsewhere.

Emerging from this scenario, only one object remains unsubstituted: the wheel rim. These humble metal elements are recycled in multiple ways all over the city, becoming the paradigm of local identity. From street advertisements to official signs at airports, wheel rims are the principal supports and foundations in Guinea's ever-more-dependant state, the last survivors of the pre-oil era where local techniques such as nipa plaiting, rod bending and woodwork were part of its capital Malabo's technological realms.

Sometimes the commons is lost by becoming unused. It was through questioning why this matter matters in a city where nothing is produced that the Akoo prototype came into being around February 2013. A self-managed space built inside the courtyard of Malabo's Spanish cultural centre, it aims to recover and give legitimacy to local expertise by applying it to contemporary needs. Akoo's identity is hybrid: the iron bar structure stands on seven reused wheel rims, combining traditional wood and metal crafts with a revisited plaiting technique in which old nipa is replaced by the newest material in town, PVC tubes. An example of how to retrieve and evolve local know-how to address contemporary scenarios.

Zoohaus, Inteligencias Colectivas, Jugaad prototype, Karachi, Pakistan, 2016

The installation built in Pakistan Chowk square was called 'Jugaad' by locals. Jugaad is a colloquial Hindi, Urdu and Punjabi word, which means, roughly translated, a 'hack', an innovative fix, a solution that bends the rules. This IC project was a collaboration with the Goethe Institute of Pakistan and Vasl Artists' Collective.

The Inteligencias Colectivas
team developed a strategy
to include these 'tactical
urbanisms' in future city
planning. It delivered a series
of visions for 2050 Lagos
that include the richness and
usefulness of the compiled
'urban evidence', but counting
on the means of public
administration and on what
scientific knowledge provides.

Zoohaus,
Inteligencias Colectivas,
Lagos Urban Commons Energy &
Transportation Prototypes,
'Uneven Growth: Tactical
Urbanisms for Expanding
Megacities' exhibition,
Museum of Modern Art (MoMA),
New York,
2014-15

Regardless of their
socioeconomic status, Lagos's
residents are faced on a daily
basis with power cuts, enormous
traffic jams and lack of potable
water. IC proposes a series of
prototypes to develop visions
of the city that could meet these
three main concerns – energy,
water and transportation. Project
in collaboration with NLÉ Studio.

Tactical Urbanism: Lagos

Lagos is the traffic-jammed capital of an oil-rich state whose wealth is as vast as it is unevenly distributed. In the last few decades there has been major public investment in traffic infrastructure in the form of raised roadways, laid out to bypass obstacles and bodies of water while trying to reach and join together new parts of the city in a futile attempt to deal with its uncontrollable growth. The unplanned occupation of the areas beneath these elevated constructions is evidence of the city's social character but also a fact of how alien this layer of progress and infinite traffic jams is to the majority of its citizens.

These below-bridge zones are transformed by the work of human spontaneity into the coolest (in both senses of the word) and most fitting public places to accommodate all kinds of self-promoted services and amenities by a citizenship of which the vast majority lives hand to mouth. Public transport garages with associated workshops, sports, commerce and street food, prayer and recreation, manufacturing and processing of all kinds of goods: an endless, unscheduled, self-regulated variety of uses sheltered from sun and rain, joyfully alive under the umbrella of a devastatingly anachronistic vision of urban development. Imagine if the fact that this would happen had been taken into account and properly introduced by city planners: would we not then be speaking about the next leap in urban development?

In April 2014, as part of the 'Lagos Urban Commons' project for the 'Uneven Growth: Tactical Urbanisms for Expanding Megacities' exhibition at New York's Museum of Modern Art (MoMA), the Inteligencias Colectivas team developed a strategy to include these 'tactical urbanisms' in future city planning. It delivered a series of visions for 2050 Lagos that include the richness and usefulness of the compiled 'urban evidence', but counting on the means of public administration and on what scientific knowledge provides.

Hand-Made Urbanism: Palomino

Palomino is a small Caribbean village that lies between picture-postcard beaches and the Santa Marta mountain range. Its community of 3,000 inhabitants is full of contrasts. On one hand, the territory struggled to develop for many years because of the war between various drug guerrilla groups and the Colombian army; it is on a key smuggling route, due to its proximity to the Venezuelan border. On the other hand, its environment boasts rich natural resources, and the populace is socially strong and engaged in many cultural initiatives. In this context, the absence of administrative and political authority led to a self-organised society that is highly resilient, but also to an urban fabric that lacks any sense of a plan.

The unique characteristics of Palomino provided the opportunity to propose, during several working visits between 2011 and 2014, a decentralised urban strategy, materialised through a network of autonomous programmatic infrastructures. Using open design logics, the Inteligencias Colectivas team managed to build small-scale elements able to meet specific programme demands: a public library, a social centre, a food trolley and a variety of composting dry toilets. Because of the way they are built and culturally inserted, all these interventions interact in a network that generates, over time, self-promoted dynamics of change, providing the capacity to be managed and replicated by citizens. Through this practical exercise a theoretical manifesto was confirmed: quality urban development could reach any part of the world just by managing self-directed policies. Now imagine what future masterplans or large public infrastructures could achieve if shared urbanism precepts were also supported by governments and their economic means.

Back to the Future

All of these experiences on the various IC projects have served to lay out basic concepts regarding any kind of human settlement as an alternative way to see and shape the context where we coexist: investigating urban technologies and practices as facts, and creating links and open systems at local scales in order to trigger larger-scale initiatives.

The IC initiative promotes hybrid solutions, the resilience of the half-breed, knowing that there are no absolute truths or pure solutions, and that a rich ecosystem is one which is sufficiently diverse to resist any adversity. Thus we will only fully enter the 21st century as thinkers and builders by being able to include the maximum complexity within every urban environment.

Ultimately, Zoohaus believes in an amplified collective imagination as to how the future of our built environments could be. And it all starts by learning from what already exists. Ɒ

Zoohaus,
Inteligencias
Colectivas,
Food trolley,
Palomino,
Colombia,
2012

The methodology at Palomino involved a four-year collaboration between teachers and students of the Universidad Javeriana de Bogotá's PEI programme, the Palomino Cultural Association, various neighbours and the IC team. This made multiscalar prototypes and approaches possible, and allowed for the evolution of new elements once the IC team left.

Zoohaus,
Inteligencias Colectivas,
Basilia's dry-composting toilet,
Palomino,
Colombia,
2012

One of the main aims of the project team was to strengthen the open-source culture already present in the community. By using grassroots techniques and materials, every built prototype was grasped and embraced by every participant in the process.

Designing Beyond the Expected in Guatemala City

Gregory Melitonov

USLY
FUL

The work of Taller KEN is proof that strong ethics can go hand in hand with just as strong a sense of fun. With offices in Guatemala and New York, the practice focuses on socially committed projects that embrace local craft traditions but give them refreshing twists. **Gregory Melitonov**, who co-founded the firm with Ines Guzman, presents three such ventures in the Guatemalan capital, outlining the research and collaborative processes that have made them happen.

Since the studio's inception in 2013, New York- and Guatemala-based Taller KEN has continually tapped the vitality that occurs when one is never completely in one's element. The result is a critical blend of the familiar and unforeseen, an ability to include multiple viewpoints and sustain formal ambitions that engage the public beyond the conventionally expected.

Within the context of Central America, the firm is able to draw on the local building culture, developing ideas through a process of visiting communities and working closely with craftspeople to research traditional materials and techniques. Embracing a collaborative attitude allows a multitude of voices to be incorporated within the work, which goes beyond merely elevating elements of local craft culture to creating an architecture with broad appeal.

Realising projects in a developing urban context where growth is counterbalanced with social inequalities has helped Taller KEN establish its thinking about working in the public realm. Striving for social commitment, the practice continually addresses the underpinnings of the field through a lens of ethics re-examining standard notions of architectural education, the construction industry and the economies of the built environment. Three formative projects track its evolution.

Zona 14: Beyond Tradition
One of the studio's early works demonstrates its approach to making evident connections between architecture and society. The Zona 14 Canopy in Guatemala City (2013), an al fresco cafe that recalls a typical garden pergola, emerged from trips to the interior of Guatemala and research of the pre-Columbian Huipil textile tradition common to the region. The end result extracts an essence that represents something characteristic of the vernacular yet is refreshing and unexpected.

An addition to the Zona 14 House, a menswear store also designed by Taller KEN, the choice of material for the canopy – 450 kg (1,000 lb) of naturally produced yarn suspended from a light steel structure – is emblematic of the craft production of the people in the local communities. The low-tech yet highly structured processes of making – the sheering, spooling, dyeing, drying, looming, cutting and stitching – are all traditional methods of craft culture that reveal a human scale in their production.

Surrounded by greenery, the canopy is visually vibrant, but also highly pragmatic, acting as both a solar shade and sound-absorbent surface that makes the space cool and intimate. The combination of unconventional yet local materials, use of colour and texture, planting and natural light all create a palpable feeling of nature.

Taller KEN,
Zona 14 Canopy,
Guatemala City,
Guatemala,
2013

The 450 kg (1,000 lb) of thread skeins suspended from the roof structure are arranged to emulate the local dyeing process. Slim metal columns modulate the open cafe plan and frame views to the garden. The play of textures blends with the surrounding greenery.

Madero: From the Ground Up

As the Taller KEN studio matures, it has evolved from representing craft as the conservation of local identity towards embracing all of the complexities of the built environment that point outwards towards greater relevance.

Asked to design a cafe and events space on one of the most heavily trafficked highways in Guatemala, the practice was able to apply its sensibilities at full-building scale. The Madero, Guatemala City, completed in 2015, explores the relationships of constructed versus natural systems in one space. Fusing Pop quotations of James Wines and Venturi Scott Brown with distinctly Latin American textures and colours, the project creates a layered integration with its surroundings. This pastiche of elements combines in a playful eclecticism to bring awareness of greater themes, fostering a critical approach towards urban sprawl and sustainability in a context they are otherwise absent from.

A 15-metre (50-foot) tall bright-red cube studded with car chassis, Madero makes the most of the decorated-shed roadside icon. This eye-catching sculptural box is meant to provoke any passerby. Despite the playful kitsch of the exterior, the interior reflects a sense of calm; the light-filled space is naturally ventilated and functions as a greenhouse. Five-metre (15-foot) palm trees, used as partitions, are watered by reclaimed rainwater collected in bright-blue tanks. The floors are a patchwork of local cement tiles, recycled building material from exterior patios. The exposed metal structure, plumbing, vents and skylights are all colourfully painted to draw attention to the building's systems. The project blends human and industrial scales, balancing these technical elements with the vibrant patterns and textures of the materials, furnishings, tropical vegetation and colour palette, taking the themes of the Zona 14 Canopy to a new and unexpected place.

Taller KEN,
Madero,
Guatemala City,
2015

The interior is daylit and naturally ventilated, with rainwater collected in bright-blue tanks.

The bistro and event space is located on the most heavily trafficked highway in the country. This opaque red cube studded with car chassis acts as a roadside icon.

Taller KEN,
FUNdaMENTAL,
Guatemala City,
2016

below: The project is located in an unused parking lot at the base of the Centro Cultural Miguel Ángel Asturias, a green area in the city's historic civic centre.

right: Entrance to the pathway. The canopy of ribbons creates a play of colour and light to create experiences at different scales.

Each FUNdaMENTAL project starts from the assumption that public space is a basic human right.

FUNdaMENTAL: Upstart Startup

Over the course of working with technical consultants and craftspeople, the studio found that the collaborative realities of executing built works are often at odds with traditional architectural education. To provide an alternative perspective, Taller KEN launched FUNdaMENTAL, an annual design-build initiative to encourage future architects to challenge expectations, to be proactive and view their work as a catalyst in producing better conditions for the collective good.

As the practice's profile grew, it became aware of the limited opportunities for students or recent graduates around the world who were looking to match their enthusiasm for design with equally engaging work opportunities but coming up short. Starting in 2016, funded by contributions and using materials donated by local companies, a multinational group of architectural student interns are invited to Guatemala City each year to transform a neglected part of the city into a welcoming and festive community gathering place.

The inaugural project focused on the Centro Cultural Miguel Ángel Asturias, a green area containing the national theatre which has fallen into disrepair. The student team chose an unused parking lot as the location for their playAchomo design-build intervention, with the goal of making an impact and initiating a first step in a long process of civic and cultural renewal. At the base of the cultural centre they constructed a large colourful canopy using recycled elastic ribbons to shelter new cultural activities and resting areas, and an experiential path to lead the public to the theatre grounds above.

Now entering its third year, each FUNdaMENTAL project starts from the assumption that public space is a basic human right, something that is taken for granted in the developed world and that will most likely become less prevalent in a global future. Each installation reflects the combined education and experimentation of the interns, all of whom have diverse interests and expertise. Students typically enrol from a wide variety of nationalities and universities including local schools, and participate in all phases of the project with hands-on roles in design and construction as well as presenting and coordination with consulting experts and sponsor companies. The shared experience of realising a self-generated project is something these young architects take with them as they launch their own careers.

As a result of incorporating this educational component into the practice, Taller KEN has defined its role in a local context and evolved beyond viewing design as a single prescribed intent, or through the lens of aesthetic regionalism, to one of mobilising people and empowering architects to have relevance in the developing world.

The studio continues to expand its purview; current projects include new offices, a public exhibition space for a genocide research centre in Paris, developing a rural school outside of Siem Reap, Cambodia, as well as further work in Guatemala and New York, bringing seemingly distant realities together. ᴆ

Helen Castle

Going from

ZERO

to

00

Indy Johar,
Co-founder and
Director of 00

Indy Johar on Shifting the Focus of Practice from Objects to Outcomes

It was a striving for social equality, coupled with an insatiable thirst for interdisciplinary knowledge, that led **Indy Johar** to co-found London practice Architecture 00. In an interview with 𝔇 Commissioning Editor **Helen Castle**, he reflects on his work to date and its place within a 'boring revolution' that proves far from boring, as technology transforms how cities are made, physically and organisationally. Notable among 00's output are the open-source digital construction system WikiHouse, winner of a TED Prize for urban innovation, and the online platform Opendesk that enables customers worldwide to have a range of furniture made to order by manufacturers based near them.

Indy Johar has form as a serial disruptor. Since co-founding 00 with David Saxby in London in 2004, he has been repeatedly questioning the status quo and stretching the parameters of the profession. By regarding architecture as a social and economic product, he has consciously shifted the emphasis away from designing discrete objects and buildings to outcomes. This is an approach reflected in 00's involvement in Impact Hubs, co-working spaces for social entrepreneurs, in which the practice has taken on a variety of roles in different projects, including architect, business model designer, co-founder, shareholder and operator. Indy has pushed for the civic and social potential of architecture through an understanding of wider economic drivers. As he has stated: 'Form doesn't follow function, form follows finance.'[1]

This led to the realisation that 'not only could you change the way that you think about architecture, but also about how you build it' with a focus on the democratisation of manufacture and the launch of 00's most famous initiative WikiHouse.[2] Started in the summer of 2011 by Alastair Parvin and Nick Ierodiaconou, WikiHouse is an open-source, digital construction system that enables anyone to download and 'print' the parts for low-cost houses, using computer numerically controlled (CNC) cutting machines. In 2012, the founding of WikiHouse was followed by the establishment of Opendesk by Ierodiaconou, Ian Bennink, Tim Carrigan, James Arthur and Joni Steiner of 00 Development. Opendesk is a global platform for local making that releases designs under Creative Commons licences and connects customers with local manufacturers. Most recently, in January 2016, Indy co-founded strategic research unit Dark Matter Laboratories, a vehicle for exploring the potential of decentralisation and distribution of institutional infrastructures to effect social change. It is through this vehicle that he has identified the next disruption on the horizon, the 'boring revolution', in which regulation, institutions and governance become the target for technological development and innovation.[3]

The 00 team after the completion of a 10k run in March 2017.

00, Impact Hub King's Cross, London, 2009

At King's Cross, 00 was both architect and business model designer. The team refurbished this Grade II-listed brick warehouse in York Way to create one of the world's first social entrepreneurs' members' clubs.

The 00 collaborative network

Bottom centre is the main container 00, to the top left Dark Matter Laboratories, top centre Architecture 00, and to the right Opendesk; below this is WikiHouse. Common activities, such as research and development, strategy and design, feed into these different initiatives.

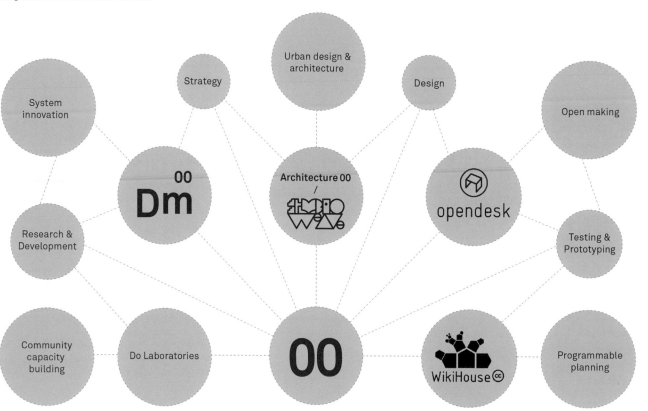

00, Impact Hub Westminster,
London, 2011

00 is shareholder and co-founder, as well as
designer of this Impact Hub in Central London,
which provides flexible co-working spaces and
business support for organisations seeking to
have a positive social and environmental impact.

From Real Estate to Real Value: Making Places Not Buildings

For Indy, the trigger for thinking differently about practice was, ironically, the Private Finance Initiative (PFI). Introduced in the UK in the late 1990s, PFI was widely loathed by architects as it required the contracting of private companies to complete and manage public projects; it prompted widespread design-and-build procurement, and in turn for architects a loss of control over the design and detailing process. However, in the early 2000s, while engaged as a project architect at Penoyre & Prasad on a PFI project, Green Wrythe Lane Health Centre in South London, Indy came to a startling realisation about real-estate value versus real value. The benefit of PFI was that it allowed architects to think through a 20-year value cycle. At Green Wrythe Lane, for instance, it enabled the architects to get rid of air conditioning and invest in the capital build, as the cost over two decades of air conditioning was going to be so significant. As Indy has said: 'No longer thinking through capital versus revenue cost, it allowed us to think through the project as a whole', which 'fundamentally changes the product'.[4]

This led to a whole new onus on real value and social and economic outcomes, which is expressed in the equation: **(0.1: 1: 1.5): 8.0 local multiplier value**. The equation represents the total cost of design (full design costs not just architects), which is 10 per cent of capital costs. The design capital costs are 1 and the maintenance cost 1.5. The percentage of design to employee outcome is 1:80. This revelation enabled a shift in focus from real-estate functions to performance outcomes by engaging in the local multiplier value and exploring how architecture might improve and enhance local conditions.

00

FROM REAL ESTATE TO REAL VALUE

$$ \left(\; 0.1 : 1 : 1.5 \; \right) \quad :8.0 \rightarrow \text{LOCAL MULTIPLIER VALUE} $$

DESIGN COSTS	INITITAL CAPITAL COST OF BUILDING	OPERATION & MAINTENANCE COST OF BUILDING

TOTAL COST OF
DELIVERING THE
MISSION

Indy Johar,
Equation illustrating the relationship between real estate and real value, 2017

Indy's equation highlights the limitations that architects incur by restricting their contribution to projects to the construction stage rather than wider social and economic outcomes. At present, architects can only expect to receive a fee based on the initial construction costs of a project – typically in the region of 10 per cent of capital costs of a build. This limits the economic value of architects' contribution and the impact of their work across the full lifecycle of a project.

This emphasis on 'not just the physical product, but the social product that underpins it', started in 2007 in Bristol, where 00 built an urban beach and 80,000 people turned up to enjoy it.[5] As the entrepreneurs behind the Bristol Urban Beach project, 00 got their fingers burnt attempting a profit share with local bars. They also realised, however, that you could not outsource risk, but could only learn through experience of financing schemes. This led to a deep seam of work for 00 that has since been involved in designing, setting up and operating multiple business and social enterprises, or Impact Hubs, in the UK and internationally. The ideas behind these initiatives were further consolidated and researched in the 2011 publication *Compendium for the Civic Economy*,[6] which brought together 25 case studies of civic projects that were responsible for transforming local economies.

Pliant Practice and the Profession

So what is 00's mode of practice, which has enabled it in just 12 years to so adeptly shift from one highly disruptive and innovative activity to another? Indy explains that whereas 00 started out as an umbrella structure with three distinct strands – architecture, research and projects – over time it has become 'a single economic company; a trading vehicle with equity in other companies'.[7] This has allowed offshoots, such as WikiHouse and Opendesk, to flourish and reseed themselves independently. 00 itself has become more focused on the outcomes of architecture and changing the environment of place towards social equity. The practice was originally named after the labelling of electronic files for administrative purposes, as it was intended to provide

the essential container for activity. Its 'disseminated and distributed leadership' still provides the vital framework for practice, 'facilitating others peer to peer' in a small office. Indy regards the role of leadership to be driving 'the integrity of the conversation'. Compared to other more commercial operations, 00 has an almost entirely flat structure: the difference between the lowest- and highest-paid at 00 is no more than a double salary. Lightness of feet also comes at a cost; 00 retains its agility and pioneering position through a disproportionate spend on research and development.

Whereas thought leaders such as Richard and Daniel Susskind have predicted that digital disruption and transformation will inevitably lead to the decline of the professions,[8] Indy remains optimistic that architects are well placed to tackle future challenges. As a profession, architects are 'decentralised with learning, they make an oath to learning through professional institutions and have an obligation to supply knowledge. They are able to deal with complexity.' Despite the global housing crisis, with its deep political and social causes, and the fact that architects are continuing to play a bit part in large-scale publicly procured projects, Indy remains assured that 'architects can have influence. Who else can imagine the solutions? Architects are trained in space- and place-driven design.' In the post-management city, when established financial institutions melt away after the UK exits the European Union, architects who embrace the value-creation model and are 'literate in the built environment and trained to make hypotheses' should be well placed to take the lead.

Opendesk,
Lean Desk for Kano's offices,
London,
2015

An offshoot of 00, Opendesk is an open-source furniture company. Lean Desk was the first product Open Desk created for digital fabrication and distributed manufacture. A flexible four-person workstation, it has a long slot provided down its centre for cables. Here, Lean Desks are shown installed in the offices of self-build-computer brand Kano.

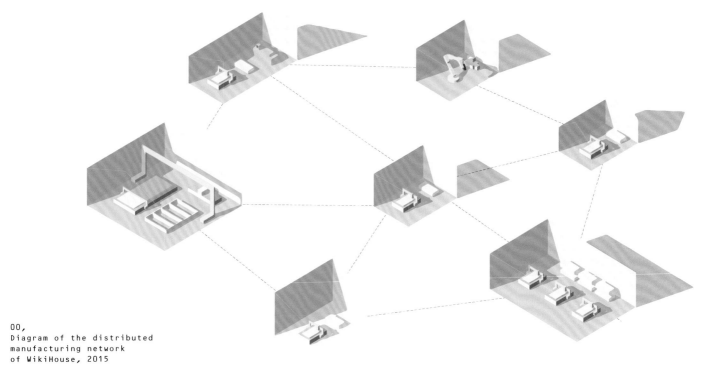

00,
Diagram of the distributed
manufacturing network
of WikiHouse, 2015

WikiHouse was founded on the belief in the power of a distributed network that shares knowledge and tools. For founders Alastair Parvin and Nick Ierodiaconou, it was summed up by an apt quote by economist John Maynard Keynes, 'It is easier to ship recipes than cakes and biscuits', which became the project's motto.

Indy remains assured that 'architects can have influence. Who else can imagine the solutions? Architects are trained in space- and place-driven design.'

WikiHouse, Fountainbridge,
Edinburgh, 2015

The first WikiHouse being constructed in the UK in October 2015, built for the local community to host workshops, classes and meetings.

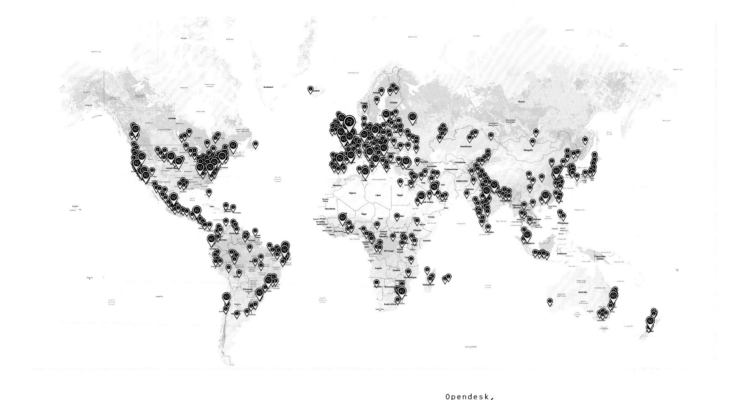

Opendesk,
Map showing Opendesk activity worldwide,
2017

Opendesk provides an online marketplace for open-source furniture. All designs can be supplied as digital files, downloaded for free for non-commercial use through its Creative Commons licence. It also gives customers the opportunity to acquire original work and have it produced by a network of registered makers around the world who pay Opendesk a design and platform fee. The aim is to make products available within 7 miles (11 kilometres) of any location, usually within seven days.

The Boring Revolution

00's engagement in social and economic outcomes of projects has inevitably led to a deeper exploration of financial models, governance, planning and regulation. It has shaped Indy's belief that we are about to experience the onset of a 'boring revolution', a crisis in bureaucracy and the way everything is organised. For instance, 00's work on two social investment accelerators, one in the UK and one in India, has directed his thinking about smart governance and the creation of foundationally different business models that might enable the funding of common goods in a new way. This is in the absence of there being 'an architecture for building common infrastructure any more that is largely public funded and centralised'; government funding having 'been killed off in many ways'.[9] When developing their competition-winning scheme for Camden Highline with Studio Weave in the summer of 2017, a plan to transform the disused railway between Camden Town and King's Cross, Architecture 00 proposed employing autonomous vehicles and releasing car-parking space, taking up 'value creation at a system rather than object level'. As Indy explains: 'Technology is about to change the very nature by which we make our cities – not just physically, but the regulatory infrastructure side of it … This dark matter of innovation is going to change our industry. What do Airbnb and Uber really do? They got rid of cab offices. Fundamental change, in the nature of our bureaucracy, is the thing to keep an eye on. That revolution has only just started.'[10]

Mutating Mode

As represented by its name, 00 remains elusive. It heralds an innovative mode of practice that requires a new level of nimbleness forever mutating and shifting its activities and identity to stay ahead of technological change and economic, social and political uncertainty. Where there is a consistency, it is maintained through an unquenched appetite for knowledge; immersion in the social and economic outcomes requires an ever deeper understanding of other disciplines: finance, law, regulation and planning. The still point in 00's ever-changing world is an underlying ethos and the desire for social change and equality. ⌀

This article draws on a phone interview between Indy Johar and Helen Castle on 2 January 2018 and his presentation at RIBA Guerrilla Tactics, 'The Power of Small: Embracing Agility in Practice to Affect Big Change', which took place at the Royal Institute of British Architects (RIBA) in London on 14 November 2017.

Notes

1. Indy Johar speaking at RIBA Guerrilla Tactics, 'The Power of Small: Embracing Agility in Practice to Affect Big Change', Royal Institute of British Architects (RIBA), London, 14 November 2017.
2. *Ibid.*
3. Indy launched his ideas on the 'boring revolution' at RIBA Guerrilla Tactics on 14 November 2017; these were developed further in 'Innovation Needs a Boring Revolution …', 22 November 2017: https://provocations.darkmatterlabs.org/innovation-needs-a-boring-revolution-741f884aab5f.
4. Speaking at RIBA Guerrilla Tactics.
5. *Ibid.*
6. Timothy Ahrensbach, Joost Beunderman and Indy Johar, *Compendium for the Civic Economy*, published by 00, March 2011.
7. Indy Johar phone interview with Helen Castle, 2 January 2018. Unless otherwise stated, all subsequent quotes are from this interview.
8. Richard Susskind and Daniel Susskind, *The Future of the Professions: How Technology Will Transform the Work of Human Experts*, Oxford University Press (Oxford), 2015.
9. Speaking at RIBA Guerrilla Tactics.
10. *Ibid.*

00,
Bristol Urban Beach,
Bristol,
UK,
2007

A watershed project for 00 in which the practice took an entrepreneurial role in their first large-scale initiative.

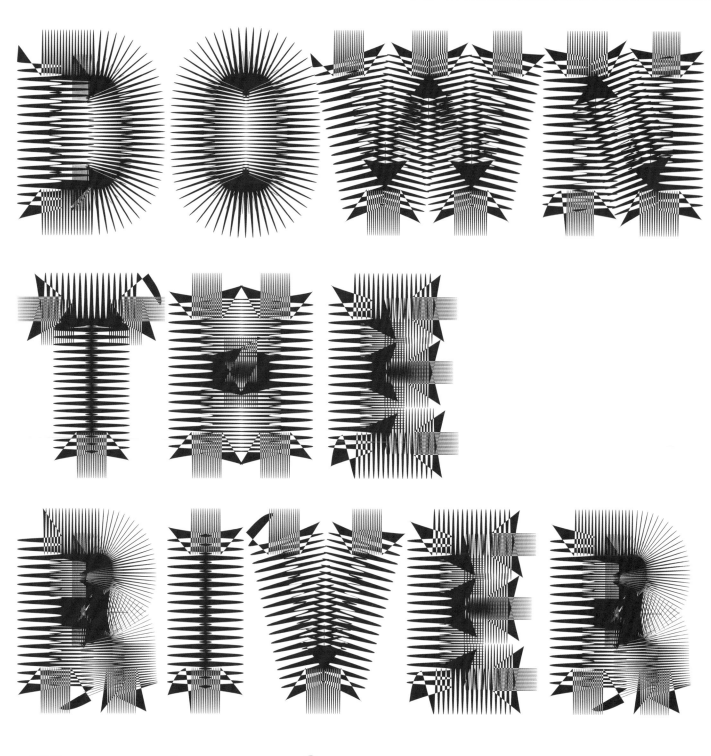

Design for Organising

Jae Shin and Damon Rich

Weintraub Diaz
Landscape Architecture,
Hector and MTWTF,
Newark Riverfront Park,
Newark,
New Jersey,
2015

Long before Hector joined their
efforts, Newark residents up and
down the hill led by organisations
like the Ironbound Community
Corporation and the Committee
Against Toxic Waste fought for
environmental justice and made
plans for their riverfront as a
possible place to realise long-held
dreams for their city.

Design is not always about imposing creativity; sometimes vision is the problem! Finding ways to weave together conflicting agendas can be precisely what brings energy to a project – as with the new riverfront park for Newark, New Jersey. **Jae Shin and Damon Rich**, who lead the Newark-based urban design studio Hector, describe how it came about: from negotiations with the local mayor, the US Army Corps and environmental advocates, to community engagement work with neighbourhood organisations.

Attempting to design with roots in organised communities – creating architecture that makes visible accommodation to social desire – means pushing projects to respond to multiple conflicting narratives. Some projects can only exist due to the energies unleashed by such colliding agendas.

Hector is an urban design, planning and civic arts practice in Newark, New Jersey – the most populous city in the densest of the United States. The vignettes below come from the office's seven-year-long involvement as urban designers and planners with the city's riverfront. Long before Hector joined their efforts, many Newark residents, organisations, landowners and others had designs on their riverfront as a possible place to realise long-held dreams for their city. So this is a story of learning to weave, not lead. Rather than mystical powers of reimagination, Hector offered the ability to negotiate in design terms, and together the team extended the social character of the material world.

above: Army Corp of Engineers construction of the bulkhead for the Joseph G Minish Passaic River Waterfront Park and Historic Area, considered a 'pork barrel' project by federal workers and requested by no organised group of residents: expensive infrastructure unmoored from social desire.

Old Plans

With the mayor's 2008 request 'to do something with the riverfront' came six banker boxes of old plans. Dating from the 1980s to the 2000s, they showed government and local real estate interests, sometimes called the 'growth coalition', doing their best to conjure something big, and architects and planners happy to coax it towards reality with ample doses of axonometric drawings, flow charts and budget spreadsheets. At one point, the planners wistfully pasted a plan of New York City's Battery Park City over Newark's mostly wrecked and overgrown riverfront. This voodoo apparently did not have its desired effect, and today the city's population remains working class, majority black and brown, and not the corporate elite imagined to walk in this new town in town. At a meeting of the Real Estate Board, someone mentioned the day when developer James Rouse, famous for creating the Festival Marketplace, came like a dowser to pick a site for the public performing arts centre just uphill from the downtown waterfront. Someone else, briefed on initial outreach for a new waterfront plan, asked pointedly: 'Nothing you could say would make me more nauseous. What does what some woman thinks in the Central Ward have to do with this tremendous real estate asset?'

Army Corps

Half of the boxes held thick volumes from the United States Army Corps of Engineers, the federal agency charged with maintaining navigable waterways and preventing floods. In this capacity, in 1990 the Corps had been ordered to draw up a proposal for a 'diversion tunnel' 32 kilometres (20 miles) long and 13 metres (42 feet) in diameter, to relieve flooding of valuable single-family properties in Newark's far-flung suburbs. To win legislative approval of their project, backers had to create a sub-project for the city under which the tunnel would pass. The project – named for Joseph G Minish, a then recently defeated politician from a few towns away, known for anti-civil rights positions – included several phases of steel bulkhead, riverbank restoration, and finally a riverfront walkway with plazas. In the minds of the city's growth coalition, this public investment in infrastructure would serve as a platform for their soon-to-arrive game-changing development. In the nearly two decades that had

passed, US$25 million had been invested in steel sheetpiling with a concrete cap, but without any walkway, bench or other human-oriented amenity.

The Corps's conceptual drawings reserved a riverfront strip 12 metres (40 feet) wide for public space. Its dimension came from the length of the structural tie-backs for the bulkhead that did not permit overbuilding. Though the opportunity to build the city's first waterfront public space seemed most promising to answer the mayor's charge, the only drawings developed beyond sketches for the walkways and plazas addressed (in overwhelming amounts of rose marble) an area adjacent to a large tract of cleared land near downtown where no one lived – the real estate board member's 'tremendous real estate asset'. Since this phase was listed as scheduled to be carried out eight years later at current funding levels, the question was raised about bringing forward its construction schedule. At this point, the Corps project manager, putting his arm around the urban designer, explained that while the bulkhead was clearly within his organisation's purview, the other components were 'pure pork barrel'. He pointed out how the bulkhead was designated as Phase 1, with the New Jersey Department of Environmental Protection Office of Coastal Engineering serving as the required nonfederal sponsor, while the other features fell into Phases 2 and 3, which required a different as yet unspecified nonfederal sponsor and a major revision to the Project Cooperation Agreement. He mock-pleaded: 'We're the Corps, we built dams and levees, not parks and walkways and landscape architecture.'

Environmental Justice

An outlier in the boxes was a fold-out brochure from a neighbourhood organisation with their vision for a riverfront park shown in a handful of photoshopped scenes. An inquiring phone call led to a three-hour riverfront 'toxic tour' highlighting past and current fights over medical waste incinerators, immigration detention facilities and uncooperative landowners. At a public housing development, the housing authority had leased some of its land for private storage of empty shipping containers, banking them up to seven storeys tall until the price of steel rose. These stacks had created a wall between residents of the development's 275 apartments and the river. It was only after a lengthy campaign and prominent newspaper article that the housing authority moved to terminate the lease and have the containers removed. This resident victory echoed the strength shown in an early 2000s campaign to preserve one of the neighbourhood's two main parks instead of its conversion to a minor league baseball stadium.

A 15-minute walk away, the Diamond Shamrock site appears today as a concrete landscape with sparse potted plants, but it formerly produced Agent Orange for use by the United States military in their wars in Southeast Asia, and spilled large amounts of poisonous dioxin into the river. Residents remember the day in the early 1980s when workers in 'space suits' vacuumed the sidewalks and the governor helicoptered in to announce the site would be placed on the 'Superfund list' – a list of extremely contaminated areas prioritised by the Environmental Protection Agency for clean-up because of the risks they pose – as defined by the federal Comprehensive Environmental Response, Compensation, and Liability Act (CERCLA) just passed by Congress in 1980. Neighbourhood groups like the Ironbound Community Corporation and the Committee Against Toxic Waste asserted themselves in the public process connected to the clean-up. The immediate outcome was the demolition of the Diamond Shamrock facility and the application of a 3-metre (10-foot) concrete cap with a perpetual groundwater treatment system. Longer term, the federal government would have to identify all potentially responsible parties (PRPs) for the pollution of the river, then issue a 'Record of Decision' (always called 'The ROD') instructing the private parties to pay to clean the river, then weather litigation sure to come from the PRPs with the threat of a potentially US$3 billion remediation bill. Back at the office, four messages waited from PRP representatives interested to talk about the city's new riverfront plans.

Produce the Public

These encounters with the mayor, growth coalition, Army Corps and environmental justice advocates, among other meetings, phone calls and field work, showed there was sustained attention to the riverfront in all sorts of ways: as real estate, as public works, as environment to be remediated; and at the same time, as scene of the city's coming rebirth. Even more clear was that so far these enthusiasms and expenditures had not been sufficient to make anything happen. Very conscious of this fact, earliest plans began as power maps, tracing capacities of the municipal planning office to push forward various projects, drawing out what coalitions and battles would be necessary to realise each goal we had collected.

Under the banner of 'Two Cents from Two Percent', a first goal was set to test the potential of building the constituency for the riverfront, seeing which enthusiasms might be linked together into a scope of work with sufficient organised support to be viable. One eventual outcome of the Toxic Tour was the offer to lead a weekly session. Starting from ignorance, the authors were lucky to be offered a weekly slot coordinating a built environment investigation with young people enrolled at the Ironbound Community Corporation Family Success Center. Together, we explored and documented the riverfront, interviewed decision makers like real-estate developers, environmental advocates and politicians, created an exhibition of our vision of the riverfront in the year 3000, and held a press conference MC'd by the mayor.

Hector and Newark Riverfront 3000 students, Newark Riverfront 3000, 2009

above: Model of Newark riverfront in the year 3000 created in afterschool investigations into the area's past, present and possible futures. The group's model and drawings were installed in City Hall and provided the occasion for a mayoral press conference and a broader public discussion.

left: The park's construction sign, created by participants in Newark Riverfront 3000 from the St Vincent Academy – one attempt to use the abstracting powers of drawing to extend the city's story to the water's edge.

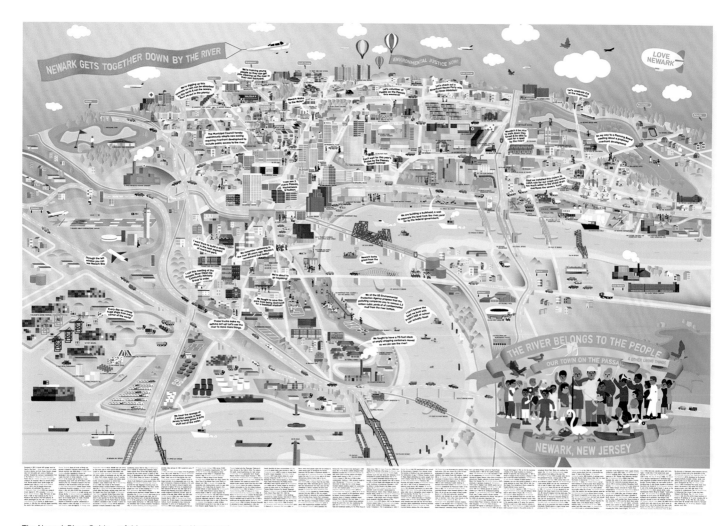

The Newark River Guide – a fold-out poster by Hector and
MTWTF that shares stories of past and future riverfront
planning and culture, and includes a large bird's-eye-view
illustration of the city seen from the river's edge.

Weintraub Diaz
Landscape Architecture,
Hector and MTWTF,
Newark Riverfront Park,
Newark,
New Jersey,
2015

The park features signage and other
landscape elements – such as these
Spirits of Newark's Riverfront, by
Hector and MTWTF – designed to
raise spirits of the site, including
its first native inhabitants, fish and
birds, industrial workers, sewage and
transportation technologies, and park
activists.

The news coverage and exhibition, installed near where water bills are paid, served as advertising for Hector's next experiment: offering affordable weekend boat tours of the river that also served as small group discussions of the city and its development. Even though logistics were complex, involving a van ride from City Hall to a large sewage treatment facility, the surreal industrial archaeology served as backdrop to many spirited conversations and testimonies. Other walkshops took routes by land, including visits to shuttered-seeming-but-active factories, environmental remediation work sites and an FBI building, which the group was told is 'just like CSI'.

These activities were motivated not just by the 'fact-gathering' of designers and planners, but also by the need to form relationships and ultimately coalitions capable of exerting power. Having experienced the banker boxes of 'future visions of the recent past' imagined by the power players and their designers, one lesson was not to expect more interesting design outcomes from the same players. Before designing for the public, the public had to be produced. This happens in both a long-term evolving sense and through particular moments. For example, after meeting with a ring of neighbourhood organisations about the potential rezoning of 200 hectares (500 acres) of riverfront property, their clear mutual interests and positions made it easy to write these out in rough language and share with each of the groups, which previously had little reason to collaborate. When they took this suggestion, titled it 'Citywide Resident Statement on Riverfront Development', and delivered it to City Hall with 700 signatures, the deputy mayor called up the urban design office sending what he thought was advance alarm. His call was received with joy as marking the arrival of a new piece of public on the riverfront scene.

The park's recycled PVC boardwalk is a stage and playground for rituals of everyday life. The colour results from a series of decisions, such as avoiding the use of tropical hardwoods, and serves as a screen for the projection of shared meanings and desires, from reversing the legacy of Agent Orange to activating the water chakra.

Orange Agency

The addition of the community campaign for open space to the prevailing narrative of economic development opened the space for a first move towards building: since the excitedly announced downtown riverfront developments were not moving, instead of proceeding with the downtown walkway, an alternative proposal was forwarded to locate the city's first segment of riverfront park in the neighbourhood that had organised residents around it. It was possible to reallocate the US$3 million meant for rose marble as an initial capital fund to entice a national nonprofit to partner to create the rest of the needed team, including Weintraub Diaz Landscape Architecture and the design studio MTWTF, both based in New York.

Since 2012, three segments of riverfront park have been constructed, totalling some 8 hectares (19 acres). Beyond the challenges of dealing with the sloping site and difficult pedestrian access, at all points the design attempts to register the living forces of the community that created the conditions for its existence. This public desire even at times entered into internal deliberations between project managers and designers, such as when it was determined that due to higher-than-expected levels of contamination, the slope of a prominent hill would be left steeper than as designed. Only a few phone calls from concerned mothers were required to allocate additional resources, and then the team worked out how a previously unplanned bench of orange planks could help manage the slope while creating a sitting area surrounding the feature now called the Orange Sticks, themselves born out of cost savings, where foundation piles were simply not cut off below ground level but allowed to rise up to the level of the overlooking street. One of the ways architecture becomes strategically political is in accepting and formalising someone else's dream images. The boardwalk, sticks, rails, logs aspire to be characters of the place, narrators of its history, naturalised and therefore politicised answers to 'Who put that there?' Perhaps one measure of a democratic public space is its ability to attract and sustain complex narratives of living together. ᴆ

Ignacio Saavedra Valenzuela

Bricks & Mercury

A Story of Buildings and Ideas

Based in Santiago de Chile, TOMA is an architectural collective that sets out to generate alternative social ecosystems through territorial action and multi-party collaboration. **Ignacio Saavedra Valenzuela** is one of its co-founders and partners. He explains the cultural backdrop against which it operates; its approach, founded on the construction of context narratives; its cross-disciplinary working method; and some of its projects.

TOMA Architects,
Especulópolis,
Chicago Biennial,
2015

Montage showing a model
exploring four specific territories in
Santiago along with their history,
and a speculative newspaper.
The project set out to encourage
discussion and reflection on
change in Santiago's urban fabric.

The last two decades have seen the rise of multifaceted and generally self-managed organisations that are increasingly intervening in the city as active agents of transformation. They link together communities, territories, resources and actors involved in the pursuit of public construction projects that recast the rules. Initiatives that combine art, politics, economy and history through architecture have created tools and contexts based on new urban readings. TOMA is part of this generation.

TOMA is a collective of architects formed in Santiago de Chile at the end of 2012. It develops experimental projects of action and investigation in relation to community and territorial disputes. The projects combine design, construction work, territorial narratives and conflict visualisation in order to organise temporary communities that allow the generation of actions, or critical reflections, as alternatives to the dominant discourse.

In times of deep crisis in political representation and collective identity, it is essential to debate the form and meaning of one of the most important constructions of human culture: the territories we inhabit. Discussing their stories to imagine possible futures is just the starting point. The case of Santiago de Chile serves as a useful example to help understand what is, today, a globalised process.

Santiago's Sociopolitical Background

Chile is considered a modern, middle-to-high-income developing country. It has positioned itself as a prosperous, stable and reliable nation. According to experts, these attributes are largely due to the socioeconomic model implemented during the 1970s, in the midst of a military dictatorship that endured from 1973 to 1990. Economic liberalisation reforms were entrusted to the 'Chicago Boys' – a group of young people who had been trained by Milton Friedman at the University of Chicago. These ideological policies took root through their *El ladrillo* (*The Brick*) – the 1969 text, revisited in 1973, that was the cornerstone of the military dictatorship's neoliberal policies – as well as through a new Constitution. The national newspaper *El Mercurio*, which had received funding from the US's Central Intelligence Agency to destabilise the democratic and socialist government of Salvador Allende prior to the 1973 coup d'état, also played its part. The bureaucratic complexities of the State were left aside, to make way for the productive efficiency of the private sector. Gradual changes began, starting with the privatisation of public industries, basic services and natural resources. The State was reduced to its minimum expression. The slogans were clear: economic growth, security and social stability. This first experiment of neoliberal policies would become a model for the rest of the world. Chilean society complacently delivered itself to its illusion of freedom. The promotion of free competition led to voluntary self-exploitation. The politicised and socially committed citizen was replaced by the passive consumer. Collective projects were replaced by individualistic ambitions.

More than forty years later, many negative consequences can be seen. Although the economic growth has been surprising, the increase of the economic gap between people of high and low purchasing power has Chile currently positioned among the most unequal countries, with the incomes of the richest 10 per cent being 26 times higher than those of the poorest 10 per cent.[1] There have been multiple sociospatial conflicts between citizen sectors and major controlling power groups, both political and commercial. Tensions between social and economic development are appreciable. Property speculation has been widespread. The city became the place to absorb capital and its surpluses, with no thought to any repercussions. Architecture became a manifestation and an instrument at the service of the dominant powers.

TOMA: Exercises, Experiments and Practice

TOMA became the space to overturn personal and collective contradictions. A place to construct a reflective and expansive view of the discipline. Architecture could become a tool of dispute. The issues of how to generate content, and how to create a collective production and decision-making mechanism, were key. TOMA have tried to generate questions to envision a less individualistic and commercialised city. A more conscious, critical and imaginative society, empowered by the possibilities of alternative social construction.

Exploration of new formats and content generation instruments allowed the firm to approach architectural projects in different ways. These included tools from contemporary art and social sciences used in various formats, including diagrams, shared meals, cartographies, sound experiments, workshops, plays, public debates, academic courses, community-serving infrastructure, newspapers, performances and audiovisual experiments.

One of the first projects that explored different formats simultaneously was *The Occupation*, developed in 2014. It was an exercise which aimed to figure out different ways of collaboration, building a temporary city with the objective of producing new forms of collectivity. The figure of the 'city' was constructed through eight temporal institutions developed by different architects and artists. Each institution created an infrastructural and a programmatic proposal, and was asked to relate to the general collective.

It was an exercise which aimed to figure out different ways of collaboration, building a temporary city with the objective of producing new forms of collectivity.

TOMA Architects,
The Occupation,
Mil M2 Cultural Centre,
Santiago de Chile,
2014

A group of people form the 'institution' in charge of granting identity to the temporary community that was one of TOMA's first exercises in the use of tools from across contemporary art and the social sciences.

Collective music production. Musicians shared spaces, creating informal collaborations and contexts to examine the possibilities for communal action in the context of the city.

Community cinema workshop. The spaces allowed people to explore commonly identified spaces in a city, such as the cinema, and discuss how they could work differently in a city based on collective production.

Community meal. The act of eating together is central to communal action as it forms an informal space for discussion and collaboration. As such this was a key component of The Occupation.

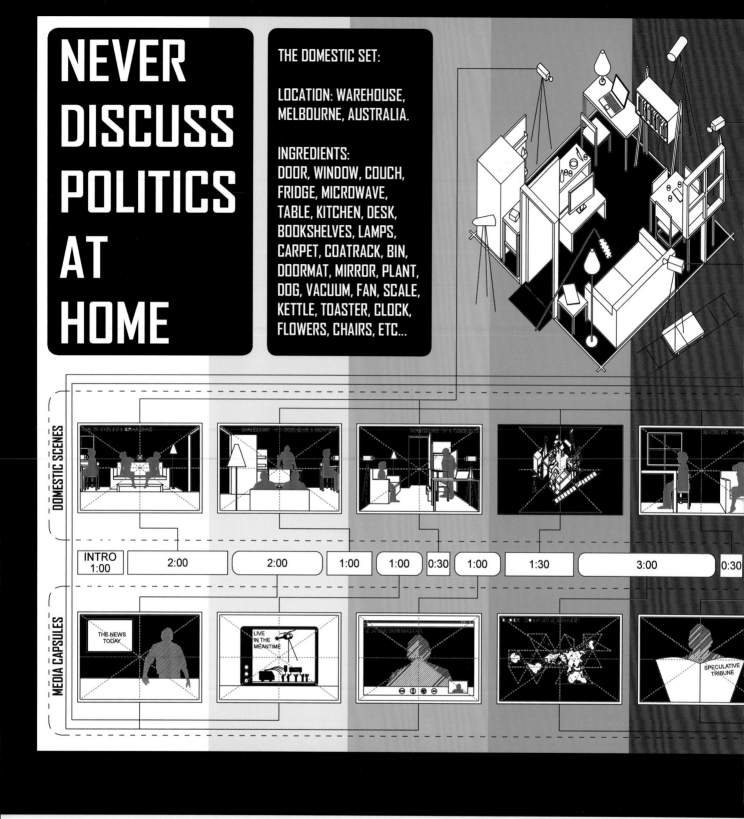

NEVER DISCUSS POLITICS AT HOME

THE DOMESTIC SET:

LOCATION: WAREHOUSE, MELBOURNE, AUSTRALIA.

INGREDIENTS:
DOOR, WINDOW, COUCH, FRIDGE, MICROWAVE, TABLE, KITCHEN, DESK, BOOKSHELVES, LAMPS, CARPET, COATRACK, BIN, DOORMAT, MIRROR, PLANT, DOG, VACUUM, FAN, SCALE, KETTLE, TOASTER, CLOCK, FLOWERS, CHAIRS, ETC...

DOMESTIC SCENES

MEDIA CAPSULES

INTRO 1:00 | 2:00 | 2:00 | 1:00 | 1:00 | 0:30 | 1:00 | 1:30 | 3:00 | 0:30

THE NEWS TODAY

LIVE IN THE MEANTIME

SPECULATIVE TRIBUNE

The project proposes a space for collective construction of a critique through analysis of sociospatial conflicts.

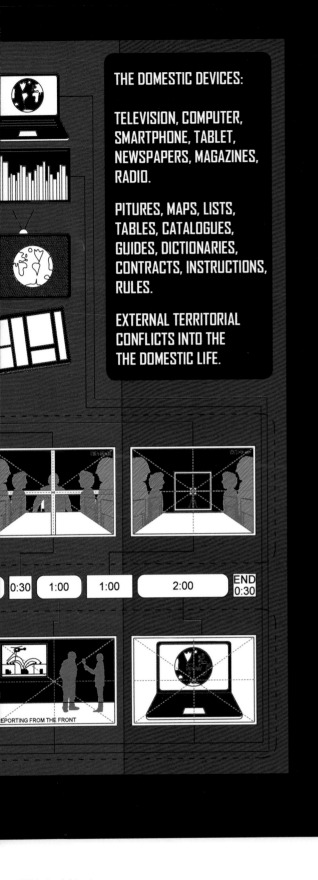

THE DOMESTIC DEVICES:

TELEVISION, COMPUTER, SMARTPHONE, TABLET, NEWSPAPERS, MAGAZINES, RADIO.

PITURES, MAPS, LISTS, TABLES, CATALOGUES, GUIDES, DICTIONARIES, CONTRACTS, INSTRUCTIONS, RULES.

EXTERNAL TERRITORIAL CONFLICTS INTO THE THE DOMESTIC LIFE.

0:30   1:00   1:00   2:00   END 0:30

EPORTING FROM THE FRONT

Dispute Spaces: Physical and Immaterial

The generation of experiments on social space production has been central. Through physical or immaterial constructions, TOMA have tried to open up spaces for rethinking visions of the future. Architecture is a technology of power. Therefore, the collective have begun to participate in the dispute of virtual spaces. Understanding the decisive role played by the media in interaction and in the creation of realities, and their incidence on the construction of social spaces, is essential. This has allowed the collective to discuss relationships between territories, domesticity, digital media and technology. Representation of imaginaries and ways to live are the first step towards creating future realities – and so, here, towards spaces that rebalance the distribution of power.

The collective's latest project, *Never Discuss Politics at Home* (2018) – which is rooted in the content they presented at the Chicago Biennial in 2015 as *Especulópolis* – examines these issues. It explores the domestic space and tests the capacities of the discipline by using the language of television, while at the same time challenging architecture to engage in the most complex and radical scenarios, building relevant narratives of the present. The project proposes a space for collective construction of a critique through analysis of sociospatial conflicts.

Conceptual language and disciplinary procedures are being reinvented. Notions of how social relations are organised, spatial distribution, themes of the public agenda, expansion of disciplinary fields, and the link between shifts in communities and territories, should be reviewed. It is important to gain a new understanding of how, when and why they change, and can be changed. This discursive construction will continue to be redefined as we visualise and understand other variants that are at stake in territorial transformation within the context of a social, institutional, political and economic crisis in a neoliberal scenario. The complex living system, into which the contemporary city has been transformed, often imposes ideas related to the impossibility of changing processes and states of affairs. Reflecting on and analysing these conflicts to encourage debate is the starting point for establishing new paradigms that reinterpret the relationships between citizens and the spaces we inhabit. ◹

Note
1. Figures for 2016 in the 'Income Inequality and Poverty' section of the Organisation for Economic Co-operation and Development (OECD) website, www.oecd.org/social/inequality-and-poverty.htm.

TOMA Architects,
Never Discuss Politics at Home,
'Occupied' exhibition,
Melbourne,
2016

The project set out to examine how mass media can be used to present some of the greatest architectural and urban problems facing modern cities. The intention was to bring these issues into the domestic space and therefore generate discussion.

Shif
th

GutGut,
Apartment building
refurbishment,
Rimavská Sobota,
Slovakia,
2014

The added lightweight concrete boxes accentuate the new entrance and create a covered outdoor terrace. The building is directly connected to the garden, providing opportunities for communal activities. The terrace becomes a natural buffer zone between inside and outside, a space for the social interaction of the residents.

Reclaiming Space for Social Interaction

tir

Ľukáš Kordík and Štefan Polakovič

nifting

e Lin

ine

Post-communist privatisation in the former Czechoslovakia has caused a widespread sense of isolation among its citizens. To remedy this situation, Bratislava practice GutGut has carried out a range of remodelling and conversion projects – urban and rural, large and small scale – that reinforce community spirit by blurring traditional boundaries and offering shared spaces to residents. GutGut co-founders **Lukáš Kordík and Štefan Polakovič** tell their story.

GutGut is a dynamic architecture practice based in Bratislava, Slovakia, that is shifting the line between the private and public domain by testing the boundaries of each project brief. The practice was founded in 2007, almost two decades after the fall of the Communist regime in the former Czechslovakia, a period that marked a rapid move towards privatisation and individual ownership – where architecture served to both celebrate and protect the private domain – and thus the disintegration of public space. GutGut has developed a strong design ethos focusing on the reclaiming and maximisation of space for social interaction and softening the boundaries between private and shared space. Its work demonstrates an architectural approach that brings back values of community and exchange into the context of a young country that has seen a surge of privatisation contributing to social division and isolation.

In 2014, the reconstruction of a vacant apartment building in the town of Rimavská Sobota was an opportunity for GutGut to work with the characteristic panel-block typology typical of Eastern Europe. This was a unique situation that allowed the studio to treat the reconstruction of the prefabricated housing stock not only on an aesthetic level, but to reprogramme the overall internal and external functioning of the building. The intention of the new owners was to create a rental block, a type of tenure that has more or less disappeared in the country. This ultimately led to high-quality workmanship and material finishes. The original storage spaces on the ground floor were replaced by amenities for the new community of occupiers, and included a cafe, lounge, fitness centre and sauna, all connected to a spacious terrace opening onto the garden. The project created a new mix of flats, with the original inset balconies replaced by 30 generously sized ones cantilevered off the facade, which became a signifying feature of the building.

GutGut,
Apartment building refurbishment,
Rimavská Sobota,
Slovakia,
2014

The renewed building envelope is simple and compact, embellished with 30 new suspended steel balconies. Enabling visual communication between the block's residents, their distinctive lightweight construction also brings the building facade to life.

A similarly ambitious project for the conversion of a former industrial building combines living and working with the aim of creating a unique community on a vast brownfield site in Bratislava. Completed in 2017, the Mlynica building design retains the existing reinforced-concrete structure with a masonry infill facade as a container for new functions and programmes including event space, administrative premises and flats. Individual parts are deliberately interconnected, allowing them to communicate with each other through two hall spaces that served the former production facility. The upper hall becomes an internal square used as a co-working space where the new community of people meet, encouraging social interaction and the exchange of ideas.

GutGut,
Mlynica industrial building conversion,
Bratislava,
Slovakia,
2017

The original and very rational grid of Mlynica's facade, typical of industrial buildings, has been retained, but opened up by the addition of windows that follow the new layout of the building rather than playing with the facade composition.

Mlynica's horizontally layered disposition separates the building into three major functions – event space, offices and living – which interfere with each other materially, operationally and visually. The design plays with the limits of these new functions and predefines the clashes through which Mlynica's former spaces for manufacturing becoming live again.

The studio's work strives to transcend local stereotypes in the belief that the role of architects is to search for these spaces, and through them shift habitual barriers.

GutGut,
Renovation of Old Gamekeepers Lodge,
Vyšná Boca,
Slovakia,
2013

above: The original character has been preserved, the exterior works involving only minimal and essential interventions such as the replacement of the asbestos roofing, the addition of chimneys and removal of cracked canopies above the windows. The original double windows were replaced with French windows, and reused to form a partition separating the new bathroom.

opposite: The proposed open-plan living space demanded substantial structural works including underpinning the ceiling and its loadbearing beams in order to span the ceiling arch. A new stove into which plates and 'parts' of the original were incorporated adds character to the space, along with a fireplace, seating on steps and niches for wood storage.

GutGut's approach on a smaller scale is represented by the studio's 2013 renovation of an Old Gamekeepers Lodge in the authentic surroundings of Vyšná Boca village in the Low Tatras mountains. Here, the shared ownership model is quite atypical, with three owners sharing one holiday cottage. The external envelope of the building is retained in its original form, with the focus on redesigning the interior layout, creating private bedroom sections for individual owners and their guests, and combining the former service spaces into a large social room dominated by a communal table and a brick oven.

GutGut believes that softening edges and traditional boundaries generates new types of spaces that bring about new encounters and the positive conflict that is needed to create new and vibrant relationships. The studio's work strives to transcend local stereotypes in the belief that the role of architects is to search for these spaces, and through them shift habitual barriers. ⌂

Text © 2018 John Wiley & Sons Ltd. Images: pp 98–101 © Jakub Skokan, Martin Tuma/BoysPlayNice; pp 102–3 © Nora and Jakub Čaprnka, www.nora-jakub.sk

Designing Up
Rebuilding Agency Through New Forms

What went wrong with public-sector architecture? In the immediate postwar period, the UK's municipal architects' departments were a hotbed of innovation, while today's planning authorities tend to be regarded as bureaucratic and stale. The social enterprise Public Practice was set up to counter this trend by recruiting talented professionals in architecture and related fields to fixed-term contracts in public authorities, while reserving a tenth of their time for collective research. **Finn Williams**, one of its co-founders, sets out the background, political and economic, and describes how it works.

stream
of Public Practice

Greater London Council Department
of Architecture and Civic Design,
Thamesmead Estate,
Greenwich,
1970

Thamesmead was designed as a model new town
to solve London's housing shortage. Only three
years after the first residents moved in, it would
be vilified as the dystopian setting for Stanley
Kubrick's 1971 film *A Clockwork Orange*, and seen
as a symbol of the failure of postwar planning.

Over the last 70 years, a series of paradigm shifts between the agency of the state, the private sector and society in shaping our built environment have in turn reshaped how architects practice for the public good. In the UK, all-powerful borough architects became derided as bureaucrats, and former socialists became celebrated starchitects. Now, a new generation of architects whose careers started in the shadows of the 2008 financial crisis are stepping across sectors and beyond traditional roles to change the field of public practice once again.

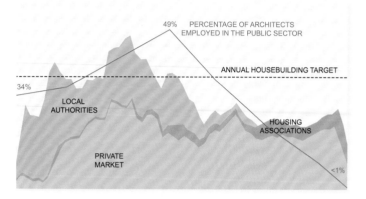

Postwar housing delivery in the UK by sector, compared with the proportion of architects working in the public sector, 2017

The proportion of architects working in the public sector in the UK since 1945 has broadly mirrored the state's contribution to housing supply. To reach the government's housebuilding targets we need more local authorities delivering homes, and more architects working in local authorities. Data sources: Ministry of Housing, Communities & Local Government Live Tables on Dwelling Stock and the Architects Registration Board Register.

In-House

In the mid-1950s, the London County Council Architects' Department was the largest architecture office in the world, and a magnet for talented, entrepreneurial and idealistic young architects. 'All new graduates from schools of architecture wanted to come to the LCC,' remembers John Partridge, who worked in the Housing Division. 'We were going to build a better and more equal society.'[1]

The 30 years following the Second World War saw public-sector architects across much of Western Europe find an extraordinary political, social and economic agency. In Britain, architecture – and particularly housing – became the government's primary tool to give form to a new welfare state. The public sector not only took responsibility to build this new Britain; it also took a leading role in defining what modern living and a progressive society would look like. Public-sector architects 'were not just designing, but also devising, the services delivered by the welfare state'.[2]

This was a bureaucracy structured to promote innovation and experimentation; that created the conditions for the kind of proactive, political and public-minded practice that a new generation of architects are looking to reinvent today. The LCC Architects' Department was interdisciplinary, bringing together architects, artists, furniture designers, surveyors and

sociologists.[3] It even had its own internal R&D department.[4] The position of architects and other experts within the machinery of government gave them access to the powerful levers of public funding, land, planning policies, standards and construction systems. By working 'in-house' and upstream, architects had the agency to not only design buildings, but to design their own briefs.

Ultimately it was the very conditions that made this generation of public practice so extraordinary – the social idealism, freedom to experiment and scale of ambition – that became a cause for criticism, and contributed to undermining belief in the welfare state. A series of increasingly radical and controversial schemes designed by the LCC Architects' Department and Greater London Council (GLC) Department of Architecture and Civic Design that succeeded it, such as the Thamesmead Estate, became tangible targets for wider criticisms of a 'bureaucratic' and 'overblown' state intent on carrying out 'top-down' and 'ideologically driven' experiments.

Private Enterprise

Margaret Thatcher capitalised on this loss of faith in the welfare state to come to power in 1979, ushering in a new era of private enterprise. Her foreword in the Conservative Party Manifesto that year argued that 'the balance of our society has been increasingly tilted in favour of the State at the expense of individual freedom'.[5] Her policies rocked society in the opposite direction, and began to systematically dismantle the machinery of public planning. By 1986 the GLC was abolished and the Department of Architecture and Civic Design was dissolved.

The steps Thatcher's government took to incapacitate the public sector echoed across much of the Western world over the following three decades. A new narrative was cast that characterised the state as bureaucratic, unimaginative and obstructive. It was now private practices, some run by former LCC Architects' Department employees including James Stirling, Terry Farrell and Nicholas Grimshaw, that seemed to offer the most ambitious, innovative and creative work. Many leading public architects and planners left local government or retired, and fewer and fewer talented young practitioners were attracted into the sector. Architects' departments hollowed out and collapsed.

The binary assumption that less state equals more enterprise has continued to underpin successive UK governments' reforms of the planning system, right up to the present day. In 2011, David Cameron pledged to take on 'the enemies of enterprise' including 'town hall officials who take forever with those planning decisions'.[6] This rhetoric bred an inferiority complex that the private sector knows best, leaving us with a system that is averse to taking risks, and lacks the confidence to be proactive. Labelling planners the enemies of enterprise became a self-fulfilling prophecy; it only made public planning less enterprising.

Outsourced

The erosion of the public sector's agency since the late 1970s accelerated over the last decade as a programme of austerity cut net local government investment in planning and development by more than half.[7] The proportion of architects practising in the public sector dropped from 49 per cent in 1976 to 0.7 per cent in 2017.[8] Half of all councils now have no in-house design expertise of any kind. With fewer in-house resources, but faced with the same challenges, they have been forced to rely on 'out of house' services for everything from architectural design to writing funding bids. A new breed of practice has filled the void left by the withdrawal of the public sector. The work that once occupied large interdisciplinary in-house departments is now contracted out to large multidisciplinary consultants. In some cases, whole planning departments have been outsourced to single businesses who use centralised offices to process planning applications from as far afield as Swindon, Salford and Southampton.

The private sector has also been expected to step in to build the public infrastructure that was once government's responsibility. We have become increasingly reliant on a small number of large developers to deliver affordable housing, social infrastructure and public space. But it is not working. The public sector is building approximately 120,000 fewer homes a year than 40 years ago, but housebuilders have not picked up the slack. Ironically, criticisms that were once aimed at the all-powerful public-sector architects' departments are now being levelled at the system that has succeeded them: that this privatised form of planning is 'top down' and unaccountable, that it is disconnected from local places, and that it is driven by short-term efficiencies over long-term stewardship. From the shortage of affordable housing to the high costs of private finance initiative (PFI) schools, there is mounting evidence that the new system is no better than the old one.

Grenfell Tower,
North Kensington,
London,
14 June 2017

The Grenfell Tower tragedy was a shocking reminder of the extreme inequalities of housing in the UK, and the powerlessness of much of the architecture profession to address them.

Outside In

A new generation of architects who were born after Thatcher came to power, and whose professional careers started after the financial crisis, are now beginning to look for alternatives. Similar to the way the 1968 Ronan Point disaster[9] in East London and 1978–9 Winter of Discontent[10] disrupted the postwar consensus, a new series of shocks are prompting this generation to challenge the system they have inherited. The 2017 Grenfell Tower tragedy[11] and collapse of Carillion[12] in 2018 have symbolised the risks of putting public planning and construction in private hands. These events have left many young architects asking who they should really be working for.

For years, this generation has seen the architectural press dominated by starchitects, each chasing clients wealthy enough to realise their own brand of iconic design. However, in the UK, a group of practices including muf, East, General Public Agency (GPA) and Public Works have been swimming against the mainstream since the late 1990s. They sought to work in the public realm, for the public, and found support in the patronism of the newly established Greater London Authority (GLA), re-established in 2000 as a successor to the GLC. A small, progressive team within the GLA commissioned a stable of practices to deliver urban strategies and public spaces, often in seemingly unloved areas on the fringes of London. They have established an approach based on working with what is already good about a place, an enjoyment of cultural diversity, and a modest and subtle approach to design.

The path ploughed by these forerunners is now growing into a new field of public practice that is attempting to break architecture's dependence on commercial commissions, and reconnect the profession with the kind of social agenda that motivated architects to join the LCC in the 1950s and 1960s. Former students and employees of muf, East and the GLA themselves are among a cohort of architects who are frustrated at having to serve an increasingly narrow public, and uneasy about designing projects fuelled by inequality. Instead the practices they have formed, such as Assemble and We Made That (see pp 110–15), are refusing to work on typical projects like private residential extensions, and rejecting the idea that architecture is a luxury only the few can afford. They are asking how the role of the architect can reclaim its agency, its social relevance, its public purpose.

The vanguard of this generation are not interested in using their skills to find the right answers to the wrong briefs – they are creating their own opportunities. Practices like Urban Projects Bureau and what if: projects are working their way upstream to rewrite policy, develop alternative economic models or initiate unsolicited projects that answer real needs. They are not so much returning to postwar idealism as reinventing a new form of public practice for a more complex social, economic and political reality. Their architecture is still experimental, but more socially engaged, tactical and iterative – on a scale that is small enough to fail, but big enough to make a real difference.

This new generation of practices are not camped in either the private or public sector; they work within a broader civic field that traverses both sides. Practices like DK-CM and The Decorators use their agility to deliver public value through private commissions, and bring social innovation

muf architecture/art,
Ruskin Square,
Croydon, 2014-

muf addresses the spatial, social and economic aspects of the public realm with an interdisciplinary approach that combines architecture and art. The firm's landscape at Ruskin Square has played host to temporary installations, cricket, markets and drawing classes.

to public organisations. They recognise that the solution to every problem is not necessarily a building, and that it is possible to design without drawing lines. Architecture 00 (see the interview with co-founder Indy Johar on pp 78–85) and Spacemakers are typical of a willingness to trespass into other disciplines, collaborating with sociologists, economists, curators or entrepreneurs. They are as likely to construct a new organisation or business model as build something in bricks and mortar. Where they do build, practices like Baxendale, Co-DB and Practice Architecture are challenging the traditional roles of client, designer, contractor and user. These offices – typically small and independent – are pegging out new forms of public practice from the outside in.

East,
West Croydon Interchange,
Croydon,
Greater London,
2016

East's work finds qualities in ordinary places and ordinary materials by treating them with care and interest. The practice's public realm at West Croydon turns basic street furniture into architecture that holds the interchange together.

Assemble,
Central Parade,
New Addington, Croydon,
Greater London,
2013

Assemble is a collective whose work has rewritten the relationship between designer and maker, and architect and community. The recognition of its practice by the UK's leading contemporary art award, the Turner Prize, was an important statement of architecture's expanding agency.

Inside Out

A field of proactive, public-minded and politically engaged architectural practice has been expanding since the financial crisis, but it remains an alternative to the mainstream built environment industry. Too often, the pioneering 'pop-up' or 'meanwhile use' these architects produce inevitably makes way for more-of-the-same development. There is a risk that consciously refusing to engage with commercial practice will leave established models of volume housebuilding and speculative development to roll on undisturbed. To genuinely change the system, it is not enough to have activists on the outside shouting in. Architects also need to be working quietly to change the system from the inside out.

Public Practice is a social enterprise founded in 2017 to place a new generation of architects, urbanists and planners within local government. It recruits outstanding associates and matches them to year-long placements with real agency in public organisations, doing work that would not have happened otherwise. Roles range from the strategic coordination of policy, planning applications and projects around a single place, to supporting councils to develop housing themselves for the first time in 40 years. The associates spend 90 per cent of their time working 'in-house' within the machinery of government. The remaining 10 per cent is spent 'out of house', taking part in a collective research-and-development programme as a cohort. Over time, Public Practice has the potential to build a shared R&D department for local government, and a new kind of Architects' Department for the 21st century.

Though Public Practice began at a time when the capacity and confidence of the public sector was arguably at its lowest ebb, there are already signs that the tide is beginning to turn. The first cohort was oversubscribed by more than 13 times, with applications from leading practitioners from around the world. The public sector is once again becoming a magnet for the most talented architects. For the first time in more than a generation, enterprising councils like Birmingham, Croydon, Hackney and Harrow are beginning to build housing, and they are showing up private developers by achieving higher design quality at lower prices.

In wider politics and economics, thinkers like Mariana Mazzucato are debunking age-old assumptions that the public sector is inherently bureaucratic and slow, and that only the private sector can be dynamic and innovative.[13] There is growing support for an entrepreneurial state. A movement is building behind a new shift in the field of public practice, towards architects designing further upstream, both outside and inside the system. ⌀

Notes

1. Niamh J Walsh (Producer) and Tom Cordell (Director), *Utopia London*, London, 2010.
2. Mark Swenarton, Tom Avermaete and Dirk van den Heuvel (eds), *Architecture and the Welfare State*, Routledge (London), 2014, p 14.
3. Elain Harwood, 'London County Council Architects (act. c. 1940–1965)', *Oxford Dictionary of National Biography*, Oxford University Press, 09b, online edn, September 2013.
4. Ruth Lang, 'Architects Take Command: The LCC Architects' Department', *Volume 41: How to Build a Nation*, October, 2014, p 32.
5. Margaret Thatcher, 'Foreword', *Conservative General Election Manifesto*, 11 April 1979: www.margaretthatcher.org/document/110858.
6. 'Full transcript, David Cameron Speech to Conservative Spring Conference, Cardiff', *New Statesman*, 6 March 2011: www.newstatesman.com/2011/03/enterprise-government-party
7. National Audit Office, *A Short Guide to Local Authorities*, October 2017, p 11: www.nao.org.uk/wp-content/uploads/2017/09/A-Short-Guide-to-Local-Authorities.pdf.
8. Finn Williams, 'Finding the Beauty in Bureaucracy: Public Service and Planning', in Richard Brown, Kat Hanna and Rachel Holdsworth (eds), *Making Good: Shaping Places for People*, Centre for London (London), 2017, p 55.
9. The Ronan Point disaster was the partial collapse of a 21-storey tower block in Newham, East London, on 16 May 1968, only two months after it was completed. The collapse killed four people and injured 17, and led to a loss of public confidence in high-rise residential buildings built by local authorities.
10. The Winter of Discontent was the winter of 1978–9 in the UK, during which there were widespread strikes by public-sector employees including gravediggers working in Liverpool, and refuse collectors in London. The Labour government's failure to contain the strikes helped Margaret Thatcher win the 1979 General Election.
11. A fire broke out at Grenfell Tower in North Kensington, West London, on 14 June 2017, killing 72 people and injuring over 70 more. The tragedy led to criticisms of deregulation, and the privatisation of building control.
12. Carillion was the second-largest construction company in the UK until it went into compulsory liquidation on 15 January 2018. Its collapse has led to questions about the UK government's use of private finance initiatives (PFIs), and the privatised provision of public services.
13. Mariana Mazzucato, *The Entrepreneurial State: Debunking Public vs Private Sector Myths*, Anthem Press (London), 2013.

DK-CM,
Manor House Square,
Southall Great Streets,
Ealing,
London,
2015

With a background working for General Public Agency (GPA) and muf, DK-CM is expanding the agency of architecture by producing research, policy, strategy and public realm.

The Decorators,
The Opening at The Fair Field,
Croydon, Greater London,
2012

With backgrounds in landscape architecture, interior architecture and psychology, multidisciplinary design collective The Decorators change places through both physical and social projects – from restaurants to radio shows, and stage sets to landscapes.

Holly Lewis

Common

From the Intimate and Human to

We Made That
Blackhorse Lane area improvements
Waltham Forest
London
2013

A spinning sign and a bit of TLC for the local
burger van were all part of recognising the
existing value and character of the area
through the proposed interventions.

Scales
the Strategic and Influential

Is there a middle way between 'top-down' and 'bottom-up' approaches to urban regeneration? According to **Holly Lewis**, co-founder of architecture and urbanism studio We Made That, the answer is a resounding 'Yes' – and the key to it is communication. By both demystifying official policy and providing tools for local residents to formulate and express their priorities, the practice has been helping to ring the changes in boroughs in and around London.

There seems to be a perception that if architects are interested in social engagement and city-making, they are forced to stay on the fringes of the profession; that an interest in people and community is not compatible with an interest in power and planning; and that a choice has to be made between 'bottom up' and 'top down' approaches to urban regeneration. Architecture and urbanism practice We Made That does not buy into this idea. As an energetic studio with a strong public conscience, strategic thinking underpins all of its work with communities.

Although the practice 'cut its teeth' on smaller-scale projects, its perspective is that the changes that most affect people's lives are not benches and planting, but big decisions about land use, housing growth and urban planning. The studio is therefore committed to bridging scales from the local to the strategic in pursuit of the best outcome for communities – an approach that reflects an interest in both ends of this urban spectrum.

We Made That,
What Walworth Wants project catalogue,
Walworth,
London,
2016

The catalogue includes a collection of incremental proposals to build resilience in an area surrounded by widespread urban change, developed with local stakeholders.

An accessible 'portfolio' format was used to illustrate the proposals and designed to be used by local authority stakeholders as well as community groups.

Community Strategies for Change

In the context of widespread regeneration, We Made That worked with local people in the Walworth area of Southwark, London, to develop a catalogue of projects to reflect local priorities for investment. Against a backdrop of urban change in the Old Kent Road 'Opportunity Area' and redevelopment of the Heygate Estate – together proposing the creation of 14,500 new homes and over 5,000 new jobs – there was a risk that existing communities could be excluded from the potential benefits of regeneration. We Made That's work sought to bridge this gap. Following the initial commission in late 2015, the practice spent around six months developing the strategy, which has subsequently led to its involvement with a number of delivery projects in the area.

We Made That,
East Street Library,
Walworth,
London,
2016-

One identified project from the What Walworth Wants catalogue was an extension to and refurbishment of the local library. We Made That has developed proposals for these works, which will commence on-site this year.

Titled What Walworth Wants, the project catalogue focuses on Walworth's high streets: the Walworth Road, East Street, Old Kent Road and their surrounding neighbourhoods. A strong community exists in Walworth in which active local groups ensure its heritage, public space and vibrancy are celebrated, and the process of bringing We Made That's strategy to fruition aimed to support this existing stewardship. Through the course of the work, the studio held a series of workshops with a wide range of local stakeholders including social enterprises, residents, public institutions, artists and businesses. Proposals vary from the micro to the large-scale, from quick wins to long-term aims for growth: a newly refurbished entrance to East Street Market, with signage, building improvements and new market furniture; activation proposals for the forecourt to Nursery Row Park with temporary events furniture and funding for festivals; upgrades to local street junctions and the surrounding public realm; and the creation of East Street Exchange – a flexible and affordable enterprise space delivered via an extension to the existing community library.

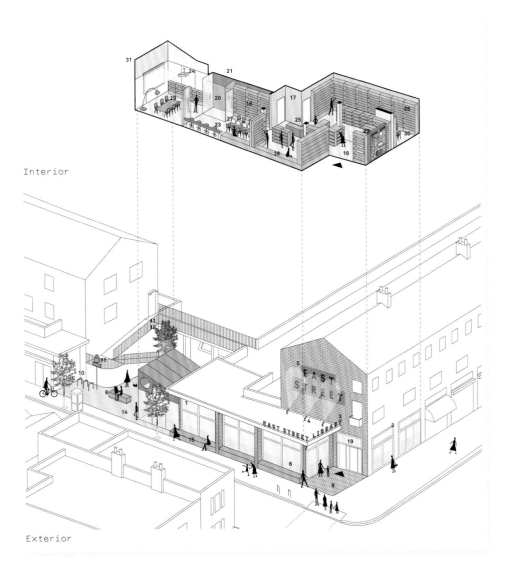

Interior

Exterior

Key

Façade improvements
1   Remove existing shutters and fascias
2   Fascia signage
3   Bespoke PPC lettering signage
4   Uplights
5   Flank wall painted signage
6   Window vinyl graphic
7   Install CCTV

Streetscape improvements
8   Illuminated bench
9   Entrance paving
10   Bicycle parking
11   Tree planter
12   Seating
13   Bespoke sign post
14   Replacement hardstanding
15   New external benches to façade

Internal improvements
16   New carpet
17   Paintwork to walls
18   Internal re-arrangement
19   New entrance door
20   New doorway connection to extension
21   Refurbish wc and reconfigure access

New furniture
22   Business showcase window display
23   Business bar and stools
24   Projector and screen
25   New staff/info desk and chairs
26   New shelving
27   New IT station
28   New window benches
29   New meeting table
30   New table/chairs

New build addition
31   New 'East Street Exchange' extension

What Walworth Wants was therefore designed as a public tool to be used by local residents, community groups, public authorities and other stakeholders to take ownership and co-deliver projects. In combination, the identified interventions form a cohesive strategy and vision for public spaces and community assets in the area. Projects are presented in an accessible 'portfolio' format, with a commitment to the highest-quality visual and graphic communication.

The key to working towards a collective vision for Walworth is for the local community to get involved as partners and take ownership for the ongoing delivery, programming and legacy of the identified projects. The projects have been carefully developed in order to co-ordinate with each other and are suited to an incremental and aggregated approach to delivery. One of the main challenges in supporting local regeneration and bottom-up processes can be the lack of access to funding. The final section of the catalogue therefore sets out a table of potential sources and delivery advice to help stakeholders navigate this funding landscape in a way that is accessible to both local authorities and community groups.

Key 'catalyst' projects that are now moving forward to delivery include East Street Exchange, a range of distinctive market furniture and improvements to buildings along East Street. Work on this suite of delivery projects will start on-site this year, although the long-term success of the strategy will need to be judged over many more years.

Combining Spatial and Economic Actions

Blackhorse Lane is an important regeneration area in Waltham Forest, northeast London. To achieve sustainable growth in the area, the local authority recognised the need to support and create business and employment opportunities, as well as new housing. As a precursor to future mixed-use development, it commissioned area-wide proposals to address issues of poor perception and functional operation of the existing industrial estates and high streets, and to support the diverse enterprises in the area, in an innovative and pre-emptive approach to creating vibrant neighbourhoods that builds upon existing strengths in the area rather than an immaculately conceived future.

We Made That was initially engaged by Waltham Forest Council in 2013 to deliver a range of improvements to public spaces and building frontages in the Blackhorse Lane area. Across many projects, the studio has learnt that people are excellent at 'reading' their places and understanding the wider processes of urban change around them through a whole range of both positive and negative indicators: cranes on the skyline, the painted sign of a recently opened cafe, increased amounts of litter, reduced patterns of crime.

The factors we pick up on as we move through the city do not sit neatly within the camps of local authority departmental responsibilities, so nor should our design interventions if we want to influence perceptions of a place. The delivered elements of We Made That's Blackhorse Lane proposal therefore included both physical interventions and socioeconomic proposals – 'hardware' and 'software' – such as improvements to industrial estate frontages and shops, coordinated wayfinding signage and a new civic clock. Alongside the creation of the Blackhorse Workshop, an open-access workshop and creative workspace by multidisciplinary

We Made That,
Blackhorse Lane area improvements,
Waltham Forest,
London,
2013

We Made That worked with graphic designers Europa to develop a consistent colour palette and typographical treatment across the industrial area and a local parade of shops.

A series of sign-making workshops were held at multidisciplinary collective Assemble's Blackhorse Workshop to support creative activity and celebrate the area's heritage of manufacturing.

collective Assemble, a series of skills, training and marketing opportunities were facilitated using the project delivery budget. In combination with existing economic activity, the interventions support a diverse and resilient local economy.

We Made That was subsequently also commissioned to assist with the preparation of a Housing Zone Bid that sets out a bold new vision for Blackhorse Lane and envisages an additional 2,500 homes and 1,000 new jobs in the period up until 2026. Integrated within these proposals was a series of economic initiatives to support the area to become a Creative Enterprise Zone, a model that has since been adopted at a London-wide level.

Bridging the Local and Strategic

The projects above demonstrate an approach to skipping between urban scales, from the intimate and human to the strategic and influential. We Made That sees creative opportunity at every level of this spectrum: there is no reason why policy cannot be innovative, nor why local initiatives should limit their ambition. Most often, the challenges in bridging between scales relate to lack of understanding: where community groups do not appreciate the power held within 'dry' and abstract policy documents. Those shaping the future of our cities do not always know how to best communicate the importance of their work to the public. We Made That's approach to this quandary is to try to demystify the tools with which professionals construct the built environment – one conversation, one clear diagram and one engaging event at a time. ⌀

Participative Architecture

The Way to More Environmental Justice

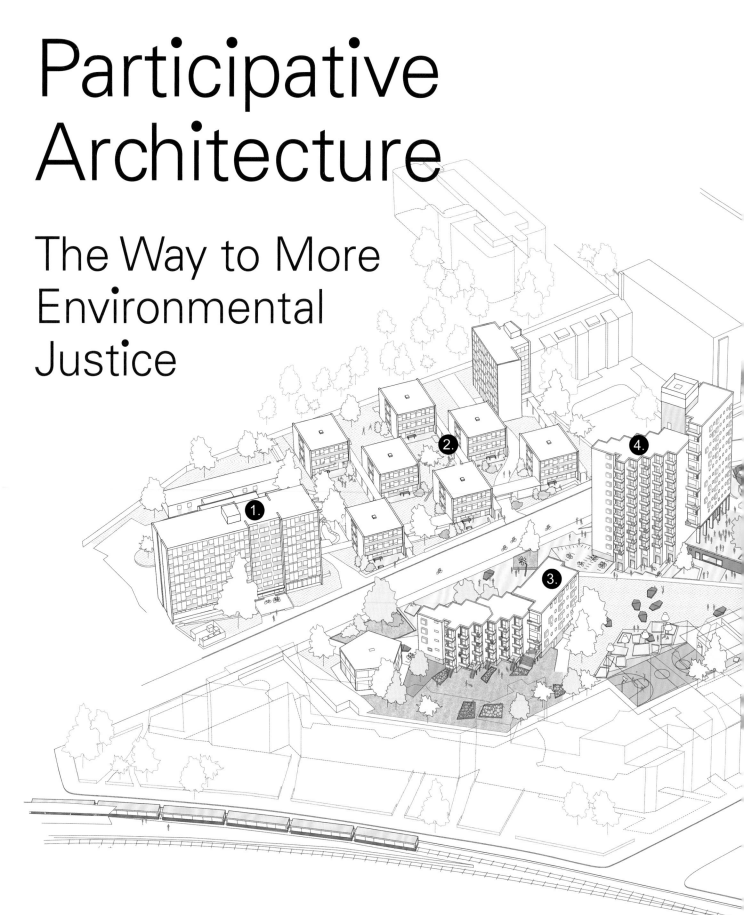

Susanne Hofmann

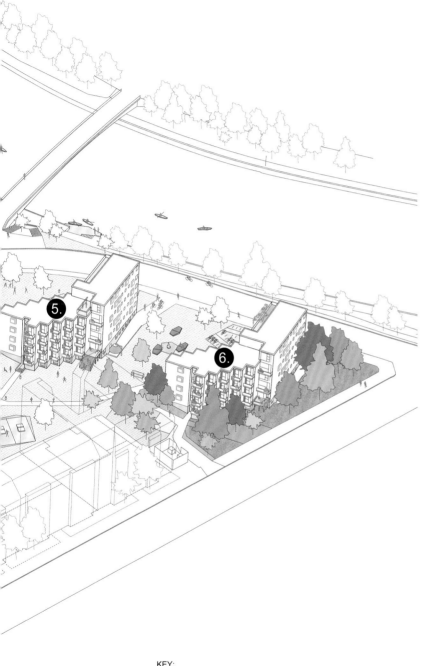

Do too many cooks spoil the broth? Not necessarily, if the metaphor is applied to architecture. As Berlin-based practice Die Baupiloten has established, involving end users in design can have many benefits to both process and product – creative, qualitative, financial, social and practical. So what are the ingredients that make for a successful participatory design strategy? Die Baupiloten's founder and director **Susanne Hofmann** reveals the four-stage approach that the firm has established, and describes how it has been applied in projects from schools to multigenerational communal housing.

KEY:

1: HOUSE FOR PARTY ANIMALS AND COFFEE DRINKERS
2: PAVILION GARDEN LIVING
3: HOUSE FOR URBAN GARDEN LOVERS
4: TEAM PLAYERS HIGH RISE
5: HOUSE FOR MUSIC AND FITNESS LOVERS
6: QUIET LIFE ON THE EDGE OF A SMALL FOREST

Die Baupiloten,
Siegmunds Hof student
residence remodelling,
Tiergarten,
Berlin,
begun 2007

Engaged to reimagine the site's masterplan and existing buildings, which date back to 1961, Die Baupiloten carried out an extensive participation exercise with Berlin students entitled 'Moving In Together', to understand their varying accommodation preferences. The results of the workshops were mapped and examined in order to develop new student housing typologies. The project is due for completion in 2020.

The modern city is a conjunction of the most diverse forces and interests, often conflicting with each other. To create an environment that is comfortable for everyone, one must be capable of negotiating and finding common ground. How, then, can communication between citizens, architects, authorities, business, social movements – everyone – be facilitated without a loss of quality?

A good participatory design strategy never encompasses merely an information campaign to appease potential opponents, but is instead a process of effective user participation. People themselves are experts on the worlds in which they live. They often know pretty well what they want or expect from their built environment. Architects must take this socially robust knowledge into account if a stronger identification of end users with their buildings and environment is to be achieved.[1] Furthermore, participatory design strategies and structures of open thinking support the realisation of innovative and economic solutions in all planning phases.

Die Baupiloten,
Die Baupiloten-Method - illustration
of participation methodology,
2016

Die Baupiloten have developed a design method that includes the participation and involvement of end users and other stakeholders in the process of design and planning. In order to engage with them in a dialogue, a common ground for communication is achieved through the discussion and definition of desired atmospheres.

Berlin-based architecture office Die Baupiloten has developed a wide range of participatory methods and tools for the involvement of users in order to develop effective, needs-oriented architecture. For each project the studio works on, its members engage in a dialogue with the client in a specific process which is roughly structured as: (1) team building; (2) end users' everyday life; (3) *Wunschforschung* (research of needs and desires); and (4) feedback. A careful balance of top-down and bottom-up strategies is always needed for the process to remain open and unbiased while at the same time target-oriented. The best scenario is when end users' and other stakeholders' involvement starts before the actual architectural design. It is crucial to bring together a 'project family' – a diverse range of stakeholders in which all the relevant groups are represented, from political groups and local authorities to future users. Die Baupiloten's methods encompass raising awareness and building a common ground for communication, observing and recording details of the eventual users' everyday lives, determining stakeholders' desires, needs and requirements, and finally ensuring their application. In this way the studio enters into a positive dialogue, thinking on equal terms and getting excited about new ideas together. The stakeholders gain empathy and understanding of each other and trust in the process. From there the studio can delve into developing the architectural concept.

DIE BAUPILOTEN-METHOD

EFFECTIVE ARCHITECTURAL DESIGN
THROUGH PARTICIPATION

RESULTS

satisfied users
and clients

affordable

needs-based
architecture

DIALOGUE
raising awareness and
building a common ground
for communication

USER
Everyday Knowledge
Expert Knowledge

CLIENTS
Economic Feasibility
Requirements

effective
decision-making

USERS' EVERYDAY LIFE
observing and recording
the users' everyday lives

ARCHITECTS
Professional Expertise
Moderation

FEEDBACK
optimising the design

WUNSCHFORSCHUNG
determining needs
and desires

visions and
fresh ideas

Participation Triggers Invention

Die Baupiloten works with communities to develop briefs regarding desired spatial qualities and arrangements. The generic School Vision Game tool – which the practice devised in cooperation with the Hans Sauer Foundation, Munich – enables a school community to explore their complex and divergent needs and creatively negotiate and develop a shared pedagogical-spatial scenario, in 17 steps and 90 minutes. The participants are guided through the game with the assistance of action cards. This focuses the discussion on the essentials. Prejudice can be dissolved, and seeming discrepancies and conflicts transformed into synergetic potential. The results of the game offer an effective analysis of the future building's spatial organisation, including its atmospheric qualities.

By using the School Vision Game, Die Baupiloten were able to gain valuable insights for the Martin-Buber-Schule in Frankfurt am Main – a 1st- to 4th-grade elementary school. The school is to be extended to four forms for each grade and to all-day education. In 2017 the practice was asked to support the school community to develop their vision of their future school.

Three distinct groups were identified: teachers, parents and authorities. They worked closely and energetically in creating their 'perfect' learning landscape. The resulting discussion among all the stakeholders and later evaluation established their desired spatial-pedagogical scenario – that the school should be made of: a welcoming central meeting place; areas for contemplation and workshops; a versatile learning laboratory; a lively 'learning from each other' island; a creative crafting oasis; a tranquillity island; and a colourful wild meadow. These atmospheric-programmatic specifications are the basis for the next negotiating game, where the stakeholders decide on the kinds of spaces and their spatial relationship for the different grades. The school community was at first very surprised about their own innovative spatial-pedagogical outcome: 'Slowly but sustainably growing independently'.[2] Only the four groups of 1st grades keep the traditional protected environment of classrooms. The older the pupils get, the more their learning environment opens up. At 4th grade they will enjoy one big, carefully differentiated learning landscape with smaller protected retreats.

Participation Saves Time, Money and Nerves

The pedagogical-spatial concept was enriched by spatial qualities from further workshops with the stakeholders including also the pupils. Finally, the studio rearranged the requirements of the school's standard space programme to establish the 'perfect' learning landscape for the future school to be built or transformed. The results of this playful participatory process formed the basis of a detailed brief and associated spatial qualities requirements. The more precisely the school community can formulate their vision for the new school, the more precise the brief, the easier it is for the architects to design and plan, and for more accurate costs and timeframes to be estimated to create the desired learning environment.

Die Baupiloten,
School Vision Game,
2017

Since 2002 Die Baupiloten have developed participatory processes which avoid the need for the standard architectural drawings that laymen often struggle to understand. They involve workshops that use stories, collages, films, images, games and other media, with the architect functioning largely as a moderator, providing hints and ideas to engage with participants.

Die Baupiloten,
Heinrich Nordhoff High School remodelling,
Wolfsburg,
Germany,
2014

A series of participatory workshops helped define the requirements for the conversion and expansion of this school's cafeteria, as well as the two-storey atrium that serves as the senior class's study area and central lounge. The desired spatial zones were determined through various exercises, and during the feedback rounds the design ideas were given definitive form through the development of collages and models.

Participation Encourages Social Cohesion

After years of developing participative architecture for kindergartens and schools, in 2014 Die Baupiloten started to transfer these methods to communal housing. The Living and Residing as Seniors in Rural Areas project in the German district of Dötlingen builds on the innovative concept for living as seniors developed by Die Baupiloten's colleagues the Institut für Partizipatives Gestalten (Institute for Participative Design) in Oldenburg. There, Die Baupiloten were not only asked to develop the architectural strategy but to design the neighbourhood and its spaces.

Die Baupiloten,
Inter-generational housing,
Dötlingen,
Germany,
2014

Entitled 'Living and Residing as Seniors in Rural Areas', the project envisions a new inter-generational housing typology that encourages interaction between the inhabitants. Participatory processes were utilised to develop the ideas and responses.

A group of activists shared the desire to create an attractive neighbourly coexistence with seniors. Collaboratively Die Baupiloten developed a vision for future differentiated multigenerational residential typologies in a two-stage participation process. In the first *Wunschforschung* workshops, the potentials of exchange and sharing among the future users, as well as their desires and needs, were noted. During the feedback workshops, the individual residential modules and common areas were correlated, grouped and negotiated, taking into account the costs and rural context.

The resulting typologies will cover different housing needs – for example, family combo, mini family, senior shared apartment, sole compact and couple compact. There will also be a community building, as well as a small workshop/studio, a guest room etc which are assigned to particular groups of houses. Co-housing or communal living can offer significant savings through the specifically defined sharing of land and resources, personal contributions and services. A housing cooperative was founded to implement the project.

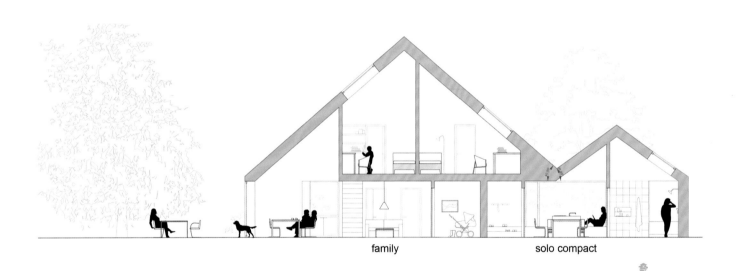

family   solo compact

family combo, 104 m²

solo compact, 53 m²

Participation Generates Architectural Quality

Die Baupiloten's extensive energy-efficient renovation of the listed Siegmunds Hof student housing in Berlin – built in 1961 to the designs of architects Peter Poelzig and Klaus Ernst – put the office in a position to implement user participation at the levels of urban and architectural as well as interior design. The design is driven by the students' visions of a healthy, environmentally conscious and at the same time vibrant cohabitation. It was informed by a preceding multifaceted participation process to research the students' housing requirements, including conducting 275 interviews, playing the planning game 'Negotiate Dream Space' but also spending an entire weekend in some of the existing Berlin student residences to thoroughly understand the strengths and weaknesses of student housing.

To ensure that the designs would correspond to the desires of the large representative user group, the proposals were presented in exhibits and game rooms were organised for feedback. Based on the resulting findings, the practice developed an environmentally conscious and communicative landscape with individual lifestyles which have been implemented gradually since 2007. Now the students enjoy planting and growing vegetables in the House for Urban Garden Lovers, and their kitchens are expanded as the 'heart' of the community's everyday life. Meanwhile, other students prefer the shared accommodation of the Quiet Life at the Edge of a Small Forest building for its tranquil architectural and surrounding atmosphere.

Participation is Architecture

Die Baupiloten have concluded from their various projects that the inclusion of the end user in the design process does not disturb their work as architects. On the contrary: the designer can acquire valuable local knowledge and a keen understanding of users' vision of how they want to live.

The architect's role must not be reduced to moderating or organising end users' wishes. Instead, architects need to augment their core competence – the production of space – with thorough assessment of needs and desires, and effective communication, to create high-quality architecture. ᗐ

Notes
1. On socially robust knowledge, see Helga Nowotny, Peter Scott and Michael Gibbons, *Re-Thinking Science: Knowledge and the Public in an Age of Uncertainty*, Polity (Cambridge), 2001.
2. Result of negotiation game, participatory process at Martin-Buber-Schule, Frankfurt am Main, 28 June 2017.

Die Baupiloten,
Siegmunds Hof student residence remodelling,
Tiergarten,
Berlin,
begun 2007

As part of their 2012 masterplan for the Siegmunds Hof student residence, Die Baupiloten coined the term 'Eco-pop' to refer to ecologically sustainable and energy-sound architecture which is neither boring nor reserved. The outdoor areas here are as important as the buildings themselves, providing a space for residents to socialise and linger, whether by playing sport, using the outdoor living room or engaging in gardening.

The Agency of Spatial Practice

Christof Mayer and Markus Bader

Architecture as Action

The standard market for architecture is missing out on opportunities to boost cultural, social and symbolic capital. By generating projects through activism rather than waiting for clients, members of the Berlin-based group raumlabor are evolving a new kind of citymaking. Co-founders **Christof Mayer and Markus Bader** explain how this informal network of architects operates, and what it has achieved so far – including local development initiatives and an open university where everybody is welcome to contribute to the conversation.

123

From its beginnings in 1999, raumlabor was driven by shared interests – not so much in running a business, but rather an enthusiasm for processes of architectural and urban production. The group of Berlin architects who constituted it were motivated by a curiosity to find ways of more immediate interaction in the urban environment, based on action or performance. In this sense, raumlabor developed its working methods pragmatically. An informal, adaptable network structure proved to be a good framework within which to pursue its goals – avoiding the limitations of waiting for commissions, and fully based on individual engagement. Raumlabor's activist approach to generating projects and work is a consequence of this.

Still now, raumlabor strives to keep the framework for collaborations as informal as possible. The group maintains a certain fluidity, shaped by ongoing activities. Soft values become important within the informal organisation. Therefore an important currency within raumlabor is commitment and mutual trust. To obtain a high level of flexibility and artistic freedom, raumlabor is organised around the various projects undertaken. Most of the economic pressure and constraints are left on the individual. In other words, as self-employed architects and independent artists, all members are entrepreneurs in their own right, responsible for their own earnings. At the same time, if raumlabor is viewed as a commons, all its members are commoners. This helps to bridge the gap between pragmatism and idealism and is key to understanding how the practice operates. Looking at the background of raumlabor's emergence, the separation between content and business was created from the beginning and is mostly still maintained today. In other words: raumlabor accumulated symbolic capital, which could be given economic value through new projects by the individual group members.

Raumlabor's interest in architectural and urbanistic processes had an impact on how the practice took shape that cannot be underestimated. It led to an extended understanding of space at the edges of architecture, urbanism, art and activism, by creating links between different fields and bypasses between different scales, looking at urban planning strategies with the eyes of an artist, bringing architectural strategies into the context of art, and creating spatial performances and performing spaces. The way raumlabor operates and the issues that its work deals with have developed in an interactive process. This relates both to content and to the structural and economic conditions of production. Within this spatial practice the group has created skills, expertise, knowledge and a framework for a flexible structure that enables them to produce intangible goods such as cooperative, communicative and affective works as well as cultural products, all within the loopholes of the existing economic conditions. Raumlabor's product could be seen as meanings, interpretations, imaginings and proposals opened up for testing and inhabitation, and less as material production in the sense of an architectural object; or, when it does involve architectural objects – such as diverse inflatable pop-up architectures – it is used as a tool to stimulate a process rather than a final product.

Architecture Without Clients

Operating outside the market means redefining what work could be. It means inventing work. Inventing work means identifying new fields of work, which in turn means being innovative, having a cultural, social and political relevance, and exploring its economic implications.

Raumlabor's understanding of architecture as a cross-disciplinary practice opens up such new fields of work. It is driven by questions about space as a cultural, social, political and economic condition for living together today – questions that might trigger a significant discourse about how we want to live together in the future and how we can contribute to drawing a wider public into the debate. Therefore raumlabor is expanding its knowledge by incorporating suitable partners in collaborations, together providing a broad base of expertise and helping to enable processes to get started and keep on running.

New Forms of Commoning

In 2007 raumlabor became part of a think-tank about the future of the Temphof Airport, commissioned by the Senate of Urban Development of Berlin. Working within the large and slow structures of local politics and administration offered a valuable experience to help appreciate the flexibility and creative dynamics of working outside these structures. It led again to the sense that an activist upstream engagement is much more open and innovative, as it is not limited by any client's needs or goals. This was a backdrop for raumlabor's engagement in the processes described in the following paragraphs, which sought to create islands of otherness as test sites for a different kind of citymaking.

The Coop Campus represents an ongoing incremental process, concerning the development of a former cemetery. Located at the fringe of Berlin's Neukölln borough, close to the airfield of the former Tempelhof airport, it is part of an area which has been undergoing radical change through gentrification for some years now. The catalyst for the process was the temporary project JuniPark in 2014, which was conceived as an open structure that could be inhabited by a range of people and groups from the neighbourhood. With this project, raumlabor became involved in the upcoming transformation of the former cemetery. The property manager of the Protestant Church, which owns the land, is a strategic partner who supports raumlabor's objectives in terms of community engagement. In spring 2015, in collaboration with the S27 – Kunst & Bildung cultural centre, raumlabor started with the Gärtnerei, a joint project with and for refugees. It is made up of a school, a wood workshop, a kitchen and a spacious urban garden.

By implementing the Coop Campus in 2017 as a description and structure for various projects investigating aspects of commoning such as gardening, learning and living, various stakeholders were able to be involved in order to promote step-by-step development. To contribute more specific content to the urban development, the frame was widened. To increase visibility, a greenhouse was constructed as a first building for the campus: since the site was still registered as a cemetery, this was the only type of structure that was approvable within planning law. This greenhouse could be seen as a Trojan horse that envelops a space which is flexible and open for different

raumlaborberlin,
JuniPark,
Berlin Neukölln,
2014

As a temporary project the
JuniPark was the catalyst for
an open, still-ongoing process
negotiating the development
of a former cemetery. It was
realised as open structure that
could be inhabited by a broad
range of people and groups
from the neighbourhood.

raumlaborberlin,
Die Gärtnerei,
Berlin Neukölln,
2015

Programmatic collage for
Die Gärtnerei, developed in
collaboration with the S27 –
Kunst & Bildung cultural centre
in spring 2015 as a first step of
transformation and appropriation
of a former cemetery.

The former stonemason's building
was renovated in collaboration
with the participants, to house two
classrooms, a kitchen, an office
and a wood workshop. Located at
Hermannstrasse, which is a very
busy street, it is the visible address
of the project.

raumlaborberlin,
Coop Campus,
Berlin Neukölln,
2017

A greenhouse is the first
building of the Coop
Campus. Considered as a
Trojan horse that envelopes
a space open for different
forms of use, it stimulates
an urban development
through spatial practice.

raumlaborberlin,
Initiative Haus der Statistik,
Berlin Mitte,
2015

Manifestation of the reprogramming as a public announcement on the occasion of the upcoming communalisation of the former House of Statistics. The communalisation of the building complex is one of the main demands of the initiative as a precondition for an alternative reprogramming through a development cooperative in an inheritable leasehold.

forms of use. A next step is to develop an unsolicited urban design, creating a vision for a future rooted in an urbanism that takes informal practices into account.

A different approach was chosen with the Initiative Haus der Statistik – a repurposing of the former statistical administration buildings, spurred by raumlabor and a number of others. Situated in the centre of Berlin, the complex consists of five buildings with a total floor area of around 40,000 square metres (430,000 square feet). It is in public ownership and has been vacant for more than 10 years. The department of urban development aimed to have it demolished for a commercial redevelopment.

In autumn 2015, a giant poster was installed on the facade of the building as an act of symbolic squatting. The poster announced the development of spaces for art, culture, education and social issues in the existing building. By using social media to promote this artistic action, the initiative was kicked off and a political discussion opened. To find partners and to create a broader support base in order to collectively build a foundation to legitimise the proposal within civic society, the initiative is working on an open network that raumlabor is part of at the same time.

The aim of the initiative is for the state of Berlin to acquire the property from the Federal Government. In a next step it will be handed over to a cooperative in an inheritable leasehold with the mandate to develop it as an economically feasible framework and to transfer it to a nonprofit organisation. In spring 2016 the development cooperative ZUsammenKUNFT was founded in order to provide a legal framework for further steps. The parliamentary elections in Berlin in September 2016 led to a red-red-green left-wing coalition as the new government. This was a breakthrough for the further process. At the moment negotiations are underway for a share of about 25 per cent of the whole property to be developed by the cooperative, and the goal now is that it will be one of the 11-storey blocks.

In the context of the current social crisis, the concept seeks answers to challenges such as increasing segregation and commercialisation. The objective is to create a paradigmatic development of an urban ensemble of existing and new buildings. It offers not only different forms of community housing and areas for public use, but also space for art production, culture, education and social life.

At the moment negotiations are underway for a share of about 25 per cent of the whole property to be developed by the cooperative, and the goal now is that it will be one of the 11-storey blocks.

Manfred Hörner,
Peter Senf and
Joachim Härter,
Haus der Statistik,
Block A,
Berlin Mitte,
1970

Situation of the disused building complex in 2016 after being abandoned since 2008. Negotiations are currently underway, and the goal now for the cooperative is to secure a long-term lease to develop the 11-storey block facing Alexanderplatz.

New Forms of Learning

Amongst the many facets of raumlabor's production, within the frame of its often-interactive project environments there is a lot of learning. It is learning through passing on skills, through exchanges in conversation, through shared exploration and discovery of an urban context, and in the form of new behaviours and modes of action. Understanding raumlabor as something that is not fixed, but an entity open for interpretation, it can be seen that most of raumlabor's work happens within the form of a group.

In response to this, the Open Raumlabor University was founded in 2015 as a vehicle to explore raumlabor's method of production, as well as actively assembling workshops, projects and initiatives whose educational aspects are worth highlighting.

The Urban School Ruhr (USR) was established in Germany's Ruhr valley, as a first complex educational format of the Open Raumlabor University – here in collaboration with Urbane Künste Ruhr, a polymorphous and decentralised institution for contemporary art in the Ruhr region. Unlike most existing academic environments, the urban school invites everybody into the conversation. There is no restriction of access. The urban school wants to be as open as possible.

raumlaborberlin, Inflateable classroom, Witten, Urban School Ruhr (USR), 2016

For courses to take place in public space, raumlabor offered an inflatable classroom. As soon as a location for the programme was chosen, the participants would first collectively set up the classroom, literally building their school themselves as part of the course.

raumlaborberlin, Inflateable classroom, Hattingen, Urban School Ruhr (USR), 2016

One of the formats held in the inflatable classroom was the assembly seminar. With the translucent structure placed right in the centre of the shopping street, learning about city-making goes to where the people are.

While the USR can be seen as a school for city-making, for its internal operation – as well as guidelines for setting up the learning environments – two protocols were assumed as hypotheses of making a good school. The first of these is that everything is equally important. In recent academic discourses there has been a growing understanding that sciences, understood as separated territories of knowledge, need intensive connections and live exchanges between each other, in order to stay innovative and thrive. The production of knowledge within just one of these territories seems to be limited and limiting. Influenced by Fordist thinking, people are very used to prioritising and categorising in any given situation. How can these boundaries in thinking and acting be broken up? How can models of transversal communication, care and exchange be adopted? The USR enjoys creating a subtle blur. The school day can start with a shared breakfast where the organising team acts as hosts, setting the table and welcoming everybody with a warm drink and a bit to eat. This creates an informal situation, inhabited by people as individuals, who connect to form a shared moment. The USR is a shared production, where the organisers offer and take care of a framework for common activities, but that is intrinsically shaped by the dynamics and actions brought in by the participants.

The second protocol is that everybody is a teacher as well as a learner. With this principle, the USR tries to overcome traditional hierarchies and role descriptions. The scheme has been set up in a range of cities, bringing together groups of people including locals and those from far away. It acknowledges the situated knowledge brought into the conversation by the locals. Connecting this local expertise to the specific expertise brought in by the tutors and participants creates a productive sphere to develop urban narratives and learning questions in relation to the specific places where the scheme happens. The formats of the USR (study trip, assembly seminar, on-site workshop and as-if installation) are set into practice in a very conversational and lateral way.

The USR stands at the centre of ongoing urban transition and negotiation. It has inhabited an empty shop in a pedestrian zone, and has set up an inflatable classroom right on a square or on top of a shopping centre. Some courses have been held walking through the city, making the school able to appear everywhere and thus reinterpreting the city as a space of learning itself.

New forms of commoning, and new forms of learning, allow us to take part in shaping the future of our cities. Engagement in such processes and projects represents an effort to create general conditions that afford a degree of independence. This serves to build frameworks for collective action and prototypes for possible futures. In this sense raumlabor does spatial practice and is spatial practice, by becoming active within a globalised economy to identify fields of work which are apparently not considered by the market, while they produce forms of cultural, social or symbolic capital that are essential for spatial practice. ∆

Practising in the Margins

High Turnover, Low Unit Cost

Aside from the additions and alterations that are the average architectural office's staple, the classic practice model is of low turnover and high unit cost. The articles in this issue of *D* offer an alternative vision, but do they go far enough? Reflecting on their arguments and on his own experience of five decades in practice across continents, **Leon van Schaik** – Professor Emeritus at the School of Architecture and Urban Design, RMIT University, Melbourne – offers his vision of what architects' role is and could be.

For those who believe that spatial thinking has a major role to play in addressing the various issues that face individuals, collectives and communities, this is an enthralling, even thrilling issue of *D*.[1] Why so? The dismal prospects for a return of 20th-century institutionally backed welfare state architecture form the grey background with clouds of bleak statistics revealing the paucity of opportunity and of gender diversity in the profession.[2] Flashing through this gloom, however, come from every contributor bolts of illuminating light(e)ning, giving glimpses of how practices that play closer to user clients than is usual can thrive.

My generation were educated in the afterglow of the Second World War reconstruction programmes, of new towns, new universities, of system-built schools. We believed in these big projects, but we were also aware of the idea of the 'descent into the street', a democratisation of practice that sought ways to shift agency from the professional into the hands of individuals and collectives. We admired the work of John Turner in the informal settlements of Latin America,[3] and we pondered the 'platforms for living' proposed by John Habraken,[4] in which people were provided with serviced slabs that they could infill as they wished or were able. This idea had a whimsical foreshadowing in the ironic Shell Guides to the country that stacked houses up on open bookshelves as a critique of strip development. Some of us were aware that the interwar years in Britain and Ireland managed to produce hundreds of thousands of houses, even if they were semi-detached. Archigram's Peter Cook was making celebratory drawings of these.

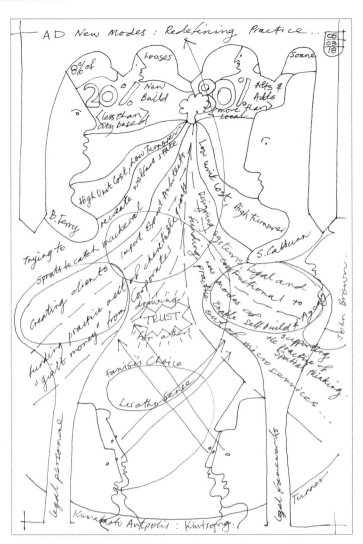

Leon van Schaik,
Ideogram mapping
the argument of
the Counterpoint,
2018

A theatre houses the arguments of the contributors (represented by profiles on stage); the threads that are brought to bear on those arguments in the Counterpoint rise from the bottom towards a peaceful tree.

Peter Cook,
Addhox – A Suburban Sequence,
1971

Cook's drawing of semi-detached houses explores how this ubiquitous type could be developed incrementally.

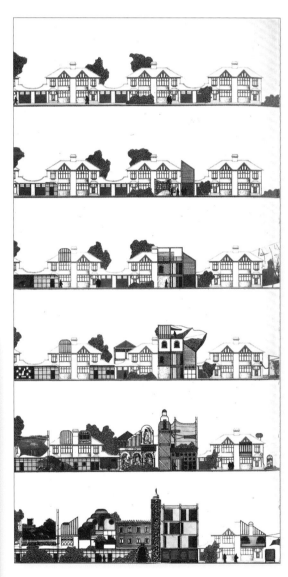

Cover of
John Turner's
Latin America
issue of Δ,
August 1963

The issue brought Turner's work to the attention of a generation of architects.

The Realities of 20th-Century Practice: Alterations and Additions

But as we entered practice, the certainties of the generation ahead of us fell away. An architect of Sheffield's 'streets in the sky', reviewing second- or third-year housing projects at Newcastle University in 1967 or 1968, told us that our next career move would be – as it had been for him – to get these built. Chatting to Bryan Ferry (a friend since our first day at the university) about our futures, I recall him saying: 'High unit cost, low turnover! Your enterprise is doomed.' Determinedly he steered himself into the music business: high turnover, low unit cost.

So for most of us began the years of alterations and additions that are the bulk of what architects did and do. And moan about it, whether in England new or old, or in Australia, wherever, as if it is impossible to pursue an architecture of ideas in this mode of practice. As I have pointed out previously in a lecture on John Soane based on an early essay in *AA Files*,[5] that influential architect honed his key architectural ideas in a practice that consisted largely of alterations and additions.

But the contributors to this issue are right, bludgeoning your head against a gloomy reality without rethinking the way in which you practice is a miserable existence. Especially when the background dream is to have an office in the metropolis, and to be published in *GA*. Thankfully not all of us harbour this poisonous aspiration. In my cohort, the late Roger Clive Powell left Arup for a practice in rural Wales, establishing what I see as a 'family architect' relationship with a county, using its resources and skills to create very locally specific designs and restorations.

Building is Always Local, Should Design be Local Too?

As contributors to this issue argue, building is always local. So finding the positive in this is a step towards a new way of thinking about and funding a practice. My early years of practice with Kate Heron in the early 1970s involved retooling a few London townhouses. We turned dross to gold for a construction cost of sterling 4,000 and a fee of a couple of hundred pounds, only to see the owner hang a Warhol print purchased for sterling 4,000 on the wall at completion. We were luckier with the design and conversion of cow barns into the Ian Hamilton Finlay Gallery at Stonypath in South Lanarkshire, Scotland (1975–6),[6] though he would not 'break bread' with us in case he needed to sue us.

Kate took a path that many of the contributors have taken, and in the mid-1970s began to act as an enabler for a community group in the London Docklands who were intent on creating an urban farm in the Mudchute (and open areas where dredged silt from the docks was deposited). Somewhat inspired by this, I found the opportunity to work with the Urban Foundation in Johannesburg (1977–86) on the design of a process for a sweat equity, self-build housing scheme through which a thousand families in Khutsong on the West Rand were enabled to move from tin shanties into masonry houses, somewhat self-designed within a guiding frame. The first acts of design were legal: our lawyers had to create a leasehold mortgage system that could cope with very low payments and very low fees. The process itself involved families in becoming familiar with plan drawing, with budgeting and with basic building techniques. Very soon the residents embarked on building their self-funded school and daycare centre.

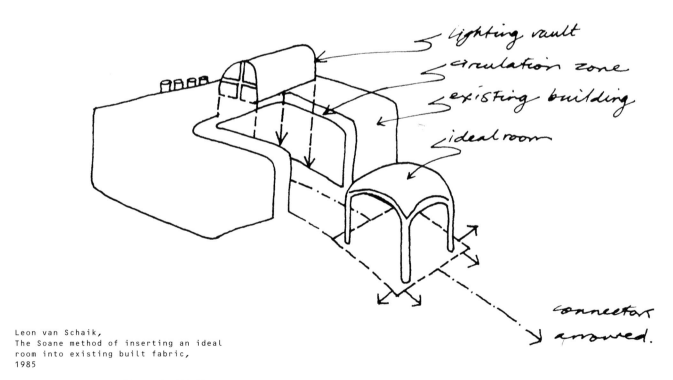

Leon van Schaik,
The Soane method of inserting an ideal
room into existing built fabric,
1985

The drawing epitomises one of the ways in which John Soane was able to pursue an idealistic architecture even through the alterations and additions that dominated his commissions.

The Most Significant Designs are Often Legal Frameworks

In parallel to this I was working with Hope Ramaphosa, the first wife of the now South African President Cyril Ramaphosa, to help community groups focused on self-education, sport and community support to become legal entities capable of bidding for land, raising and holding funds, and applying for matching funding for the facilities they wanted to create. Chief among these was the Funda Centre in Soweto, outside Johannesburg (1983), a campus for mathematics and science clubs, for language and theatre groups. What can I carry forward from this into the realms that the contributors to this ⌂ reveal? We had great difficulty with the perceptions of managers and senior social workers who would argue that they knew what people wanted – everyone was the same – and that our processes were wasteful.

Never Underestimate the Contribution to Design that the Usually Designed-For Can Make

Yet in 1988, as part of my PhD,[7] I studied a thousand house plans created by a thousand families at Khutsong on the reef near Johannesburg, and found that although there were a dozen basic themes, no two plans were identical. This is in a sense the nub of these alternative modes of practice: expertise is developed and put to the service of observing and listening within collectives and communities. In shorthand, this approach trusts people to know what is best for them. It does not foist solutions onto them.

As part of my work for the Urban Foundation in the late 1980s and early 1990s, I assisted in a forensic analysis of what went wrong with a World Bank-funded housing project in Maseru, Lesotho. A handsome row of terraced houses was supposed to stem the low-density sprawl of the city. But there were no takers. We interviewed people who might have been purchasers or tenants, and found that they had a clear understanding of the economic trap that these townhouses were. 'You see,' they said, 'our economy is tied to the boom-and-bust cycle of the mining industry. We need land to buffer the bad times that always follow good times. So we wait to get an allocation of a quarter acre from our clan leader. Then we build a lean-to on one boundary at the street edge. We plant fruit trees, and grow maize and vegetables. During slack times on the mines the men build another lean-to, we move into it and rent out the first one. Eventually we reach the back corner and make an "L" shape for our permanent home. Meantime while the men are away we women all tend the land, care for the children, share domestic chores. How could we manage in a townhouse?'

Thwarting of New Modes of Practice

I would be cautious about the 'sprats to catch a mackerel' notion that being successful in community or collective enabling is the first step towards a practice in which high design can come into play, a kind of self-sabotage of 'being in the street' in favour of playing the aesthetic games of iconic architecture. And never underestimate the cunning with which those whose professional identity is threatened by your success will work to thwart you. Shortly after arriving in Australia in 1987 I discovered that a self-build, sweat-equity programme created by an indigenous community in New South Wales had been torpedoed by bureaucrats who

'What inspires me about this ⌂, despite my awareness that much of what is being done is supported by government agencies that may well withdraw their support when the politics shift, is the idea of practitioners being 'guides to the built environment'.'

declared the crushing strength of the bricks being made substandard. And this for single-storey construction.

What inspires me about this ⌂, despite my awareness that much of what is being done is supported by government agencies that may well withdraw their support when the politics shift, is the idea of practitioners being 'guides to the built environment'. One of the major battles I fought and lost was to get recognition for the hundreds of builders working in the townships of South Africa providing a one-stop service: plan drawing, budgeting, constructing. They struggled with technical issues: How do you build a foundation that is part on rock, part on sand? How do you avoid leaking gutters between existing roofs and extension roofs? But with very little effort, systematic guidance could have been provided, to the benefit of clients and practitioners.

Acupuncture Rather than Masterplanning

In the 1990s, the Kumamoto Artpolis in Japan pioneered an acupuncture approach to urban and regional renewal, eschewing masterplanning in favour of projects that built upon local traditions and practices.[8] An annual puppet festival in the mountains became the focus for a puppetry school and factory. The ephemera from annual festivals became a museum attracting visitors to a remote valley. Public toilets were constructed at scenic sites. An observatory was extended. Bridges were repaired and new bridges built. Of course this was an enlightened act by a prefecture governor and an unusually self-effacing consultant architect (Arata Isozaki). But contributions here show how the idea of a multitude of small interventions within and supportive of local commons can transform a place and its economic situation.

A High Turnover/Low Unit Cost Future for Practice

Is there a future for such micro-practices? What I see in the contributions to this *D* is a future in which architectural thinking, spatial intelligence, is provided to communities from within on a micro scale with a myriad of fee-for-service payments: high turnover, low unit cost. Reading between the lines I get the sense that most of these contributors find that being embedded in collectives, in communities, is immensely rewarding, feeds their sense of self-worth and gives meaning to their lives.

During my 30 years of research with architects into the nature of their mastery[9] I have encountered many different modes of practice, many different ways of surviving and thriving. In the context of this *D*, the ability to create work where none seems to exist comes to mind. During a financial crisis, the six staff working for the principals of Antwerp-based import.export Architects challenged them to create work so that the studio could continue. They combed newspapers for any and every tender, finding one for lighting the sewers of the city so that tourists could be boated about the system. They put in a winning tender that placed safety-helmet-mounted lamps on every tourist who would walk the tunnels in wellington boots and safety garb, and submitted a design-and-construction cost for a visitor-induction and changing room. Which has been beautifully realised. This was the first of many such laterally creative enterprises.

Sarah Calburn, a Johannesburg-based architect whose skills I greatly admire, has created numerous wonderful houses for clients of the more fortunate kind. Recently she has become a little wary of this career. She now offers a service in which for a small fee she will help families assess their situations, plan a future trajectory for their passage through life, and plot ways to achieve this anywhere in the region. She has transformed herself from a high unit cost/low turnover architect always living on the edge of cash-flow interruption into a high turnover/low unit cost professional with a far deeper impact on the lives of the people in her community.

I get the sense that most of these contributors find that being embedded in collectives, in communities, is immensely rewarding, feeds their sense of self-worth and gives meaning to their lives.

import.export Architecture,
RUI.MTE,
Antwerp,
Belgium,
2006

In this project for opening up the sewers of the city to tourists, the Antwerp practice embarked on a trajectory of radically reinterpreting briefs, a strategy that included tendering for work not obviously intended for architects.

```
i    reception, information, ticket office
1    guide room
2    boots for visitor groups
3    sanitary facilities
4    cover of historical well
5    oufits for visitor groups
6    film 'de Antwerpse ruien' (8 minutes)
7    historical basement opening
8    historical street basement (c. XVI cen.), currently basement room
9    ruien-entrance (2005)
10   ruien wall, including old city wall (XII cen.)
11   telescope with view to:
     A    shipwreck of the old ruien-boat (c. 1900-2006)
     B    crocodile (sometimes)
     C    border for improved canalisation (c. 1872)
     D    kordewagenkruiersbrug (remnant)
     E    septum of the discharge to the Schelde river
          (distance to the Scheldekaai: 175 m)
     F    waterbasin: 123 length, 75 cm depth (2005)
12   passarelle (2005, glass fibre reinforced plastic) with view to:
     G    street sign Suiker Rui (1880, lavasteen + email)
     H    depth indicators (2007)
     I    calcium deposits and salt crystals (glintings)
     J    ring (for the maintenance dingy)
     K    under water: drain pipes in polyester (2006)
     L    connection of wastewater to drain pipes
     M    plant growth with artificial lighting (since 2005)
     N    vault (XIX cen., partially since XVI cen.)
13   island: departure of the boat tour
     O    new ruien- boat 'Ludo I' (2006)
     P    pit cover in vault
     Q    street sign Gildenkamerstraat
     R    drain pipe from city
```

+7.73m SPRING TIDE 1953
+7.00m STONE ANKERS SCHELDEKAAI

+5.84m TOP OF VAULT UNDER SUIKERRUI
+5.24m HIGH TIDE SCHELDE (average)*

+1.54m BOTTOM OF RUIEN

+0.05m LOW TIDE SCHELDER (average)
+5.24m SEA LEVEL OOSTENDE

In Calgary, Canada, John Brown's Housebrand residential architecture and construction company has been working on how to broaden the reach of architecture beyond the 8 per cent of houses that are bespoke designed and into the median-income areas of suburban infill and renewal. The latest iteration of this involves the provision of care units that can be craned into suburban yards to enable the elderly to age in place with full medical support.

In our book *Suburbia Re-Imagined* (2018),[10] Nigel Bertram and I explore the possibility of working in the spaces surrounding large regional infrastructures such as universities, hospitals, shopping centres and airports to leverage into existence new facilities for those ageing in place, as well as those caring for young families.

As this 𝕯 demonstrates, alternative modes of practice await. All you have to do is give up on what you think practice ought to be. 𝕯

Notes
1. For more on spatial thinking, see Leon van Schaik, *Spatial Intelligence: New Futures for Architecture*, John Wiley & Sons (Chichester), 2008.
2. See Douglas Murphy's article on 'Constitutive Crises' on pp 14–21 of this issue.
3. John FC Turner, *Freedom to Build*, Colliers MacMillan (New York), 1972, and Turner, 'Housing by People', in Martin Spring and Haig Beck (eds), 𝕯 Autonomous Houses, vol XLVI, Spring 1976, pp 8–11.
4. N John Habraken, *Supports: An Alternative to Mass Housing*, Architectural Press (London), 1972.
5. Leon van Schaik, 'Walls, Toys and the "Ideal" Room: An Analysis of the Architecture of Sir John Soane', *AA Files*, 9, Summer 1985, pp 45–53.
6. Lance Wright, 'Gallery at Dunsyre; architects Heron van Schaik', *Architectural Review*, XIII (972), February 1978, pp 86–9.
7. Leon van Schaik, 'Context and Value Thresholds as Demonstrated in Certain Southern African Assisted and Self-Help Housing', 1988.
8. Leon van Schaik, *Procuring Innovative Architecture*, Routledge (London), 2010, pp 36–40.
9. For more on this research programme, see Leon van Schaik, *Mastering Architecture: Becoming a Creative Innovator in Practice*, John Wiley & Sons (Chichester), 2005, and van Schaik, *Practical Poetics in Architecture*, John Wiley & Sons (Chichester), 2015.
10. Leon van Schaik and Nigel Bertram, *Suburbia Re-Imagined: Ageing and Increasing Populations in the Low-Rise City*, Routledge (New York), 2018.

Housebrand,
Future Adaptive Building
for Ageing in Place,
Calgary,
Canada,
2018

Plan and photograph of a craned-in unit constructed by John Brown's company Housebrand. This rented-out unit meets full hospital care requirements and can be located in any suburban backyard. A new way of providing affordable and accessible care arising from a new mode of practice.

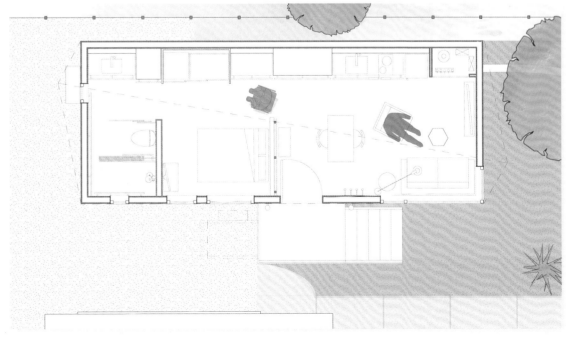

CONTRIBUTORS

Alex Axinte is an architect working and living in Bucharest. He graduated in 2004 from the Ion Mincu University of Architecture and Urbanism. In 2006 he co-founded architectural studio and public space practice studioBASAR with Cristi Borcan. He is currently undertaking an MA in Social Sciences as part of a PhD by practice at the University of Sheffield, UK.

Markus Bader studied architecture in Berlin and London. He graduated in 1996 at the Bartlett School of Architecture, University College London (UCL). In 1999 he co-founded raumlaborberlin. HIs academic activities include guest professorships in Düsseldorf, Kassel and Prague, complemented by many workshops and lectures held internationally. He is also a professor at the Berlin University of the Arts.

Cristi Borcan is a Bucharest-based architect and co-founder of studioBASAR, which initiates and develops actions and projects within public space. In 2017 studioBASAR was one of the honorees of the Social Design Circle awarded by the Curry Stone Foundation, and in 2018 a recipient of the National Cultural Fund Award.

Shumi Bose is a teacher, curator and editor based in London. She is Senior Lecturer and Coordinator of Contextual Studies in Architecture at Central Saint Martins College of Art and Design. She is also a curator of exhibitions at the Royal Institute of British Architects (RIBA). She curated 'Pablo Bronstein: Conservatism, or The Long Reign of Pseudo Georgian Architecture' at the RIBA in 2017. She also co-curated 'Home Economics', for the British Pavilion at the 2016 Venice Architecture Biennale. Recent publications include *Home Economics* (The Spaces, 2016) and *Wherever You Find People: The Radical Schools of Oscar Niemeyer, Leonel Brizola and Darcy Ribeiro* (with Aberrant Architecture; Park Books, 2016).

Juan Chacón Gragera is a Spanish architect based in Berlin and Athens, and co-founder of Zoohaus Collective, whose main research project, Inteligencias Colectivas, was exhibited at the Museum of Modern Art (MoMA) in New York and MAK – Museum of Applied Arts in Vienna. He graduated from the Escuela Técnica Superior de Arquitectura de Madrid (ETSAM), and is also a co-founder and associate member of the Zuloark open office. His activities include the development of projects based on collaborative environments and co-responsibility professional models. He has been involved in different internationally renowned grassroots projects such as the Campo de Cebada open-air community space, which received the Prix Ars Electronica Golden Nica award.

Manuel Domínguez Fernández is a Spanish architect based in La Coruña and Barcelona, and a co-founder of the Zoohaus Collective. He graduated from ETSAM in Madrid, and works in the fields of distributed urbanism, focusing on 'middle-out' solutions and the qualitative innovation of their theoretical and practical basis. He is a Zuloark studio associate, and lectures at schools and cultural institutions such as the Goethe-Institut in Berlin, Architektüros Fondas in Vilnius, FAD association in Barcelona, and the Serpentine Gallery, London. He is a guest professor at Tamkang University in Taipei, Escuela Técnica Superior de Arquitectura (ESARQ) at the International University of Catalonia and Escola Massana in Barcelona, and Soongsil University in Seoul.

Susanne Hofmann is the founder and director of Berlin architecture office Die Baupiloten BDA, an interdisciplinary practice specialising in educational, cultural and housing projects as well as socially engaged urban development generated through unique participatory design strategies. The practice's work focuses on innovative experimental design that is driven by both a social and ecological agenda. For her PhD, she researched and developed 'atmosphere as a participatory planning strategy', which was expanded upon in the book *Architecture is Participation* (Jovis Verlag, 2014). She has held international teaching positions in London, Melbourne, Auckland, Sheffield, Berlin and Vienna.

Indy Johar is a trained and registered architect. Over the course of the last 15 years he has co-founded and established an RIBA London Building of the Year award-winning architectural practice, Architecture 00. On behalf of 00, he has co-founded multiple social start-up accelerators and Impact Hubs in the UK, while supporting the development of open-source manufacturing ventures in London – from Open Desk to WikiHouse – and most recently founding Dark Matter. He is also a Fellow of the Royal Society for the Encouragement of Arts, Manufactures and Commerce (RSA), a United Nations Development Programme (UNDP) Innovation Facility Advisory Board Member and an RIBA Council Member. He was a member of the Mayor of London's SME Working Group, Inclusive Growth Commissioner for the RSA, Advisor to the Joseph Rowntree Foundation (JRF) Anti-Poverty Commission, and has most recently been appointed a member of the Mayor of London's Good Growth By Design panel and a Young Foundation Senior Innovation Associate.

Alison Killing is an architect, urban designer and documentary maker based in Rotterdam, where she runs her own studio, Killing Architects. Her work is about using architecture, urban planning, data and mapping to tell urgent stories. These range from the ways in which death has shaped our cities over the past 100 years, to narratives of migration to Europe and the refugee 'crisis', to how we attempt to reconstruct our cities after disaster. She finds innovative ways to connect people with their built environment, how it works, and how it might be different in future, using exhibitions, events, writing and film. She is a TED Fellow and WIRED Innovation Fellow.

Lukáš Kordík is an architect and urbanist. He graduated from the Slovak University of Technology in Bratislava, where he has also worked as a visiting lecturer. He was also previously a teaching assistant in the Department of Architecture at the Academy of Fine Arts and Design in Bratislava. He is a co-founder of architecture practice GutGut, where he primarily focuses on the subject of moving boundaries between private and public space within various scales and typologies. He also is a co-founder of the Office for Collaborative Architects (OFCA), an informal collective of architects who share their knowledge and expertise that is a continuation of the City Visions Europe exchange programme. He frequently gives lectures about his work in Slovakia and abroad.

Holly Lewis co-founded architecture and urbanism practice We Made That in 2006. She has led a unique range of urban projects for the practice, from pioneering industrial intensification work through to comprehensive high-street regeneration. She also leads the practice's research portfolio, which has included studies of local economies and placemaking across London. She is a registered architect and affiliate member of the Landscape Institute. She was shortlisted for the AJ Emerging Woman Architect of the Year Award 2012, and is appointed as a CABE Built Environment Expert and a Mayor's Design Advocate for the Greater London Authority.

Brian McGrath is Professor of Urban Design and former Dean of the School of Constructed Environments at the Parsons School of Design in New York. His books include the *∆* Reader *Urban Design Ecologies* (John Wiley & Sons, 2012), *Resilience in Ecology and Urban Design* (Springer, 2012), *Digital Modelling for Urban Design* (John Wiley & Sons, 2008), *Cinemetrics: Architectural Drawing Today* (John Wiley & Sons, 2007) and *Transparent Cities* (Lumen, 1994). He is a Principal Investigator for the Baltimore Ecosystem Study, served as a Fulbright Senior Scholar in Thailand from 1998 to 1999, and was an India China Institute Fellow from 2006 to 2008.

Christof Mayer studied architecture in Berlin and London. He graduated in 1998 from the Technical University of Berlin. In 1999 he co-founded raumlaborberlin. He teaches internationally, supplemented by numerous lectures. In 2014 he held the presidency at the Monash University in Melbourne. Since 2017 he has been a professor at the Bergen Architecture School in Norway. He is also a guest professor at the Berlin University of the Arts.

Gregory Melitonov received his Master of Architecture from Yale University in New Haven, Connecticut, and his Bachelor of Science from Skidmore College in Saratoga Springs, New York. Prior to co-founding Guatemala-based studio Taller KEN with Ines Guzman in 2013, he worked for Renzo Piano as part of the design team for the Whitney Museum of American Art in New York City. His independent research revolves around architecture and the role of the architect in the public realm. He has previously taught at the Universidad Francisco Marroquín in Guatemala, New York Institute of Technology and the School of Visual Arts in New York City.

Douglas Murphy writes for a wide variety of publications on architecture, art, politics and culture, teaches in the architecture departments of the Royal College of Art (RCA) and Central Saint Martins in London, and lectures widely throughout Europe. His most recent book is *Nincompoopolis* (Repeater, 2017), telling the story of the architectural meddlings of Boris Johnson, the last mayor of London. He is also the author of *Last Futures: Nature, Technology and the End of Architecture* (Verso, 2016) and *The Architecture of Failure* (Zero, 2012).

Constantin Petcou is a Paris-based architect whose work stresses the intersection between architecture, urbanism, service design and semiotics. He is the co-founder, with Doina Petrescu, of atelier d'architecture autogérée (aaa), a professional organisation that conducts actions and research on participatory urbanism and architecture (urbantactics. org). aaa's projects include Ecobox, and Passage 56, and more recently R-Urban, a participative strategy of urban resilience in the Parisian region and London, and the Wiki Village Factory, a cluster for social and ecological innovation in Paris. The office's work has received numerous international awards including the Innovation in Politics Award, Zumtobel, Curry Stone and European Public Space prizes.

Doina Petrescu is Professor of Architecture and Design Activism at the University of Sheffield, and co-founder of atelier d'architecture autogérée (aaa). Her cross-disciplinary research addresses outstanding questions in architecture and urban planning, focusing on issues of civic participation and gender and the relations between coproduction, urban commons and resilience. Her publications include *The Social (Re)Production of Architecture* (Routledge, 2016), *Learn to Act* (Peprav/aaa, 2017), *Altering Practices: Feminist Politics and Poetics of Space* (Routledge, 2007) and *Architecture and Participation* (Routledge, 2005). She is currently working on the book *Architecture Otherhow: Questioning Contemporary Practice* (Routledge, 2019).

Štefan Polakovič is an architect and co-founder of GutGut. He has an extensive portfolio of expertise in a number of fields. His innovative approach to work surpasses traditional solutions. His project Ťahanovce, a functional and typological design for residential estate structure near Košice town, won the Europan 5: New Housing Landscape, Travel and Proximity award. He is Head of the Public Buildings Department at the Faculty of Architecture, Slovak University of Technology in Bratislava, and works as a co-organiser of the Days of Architecture and Design (DAAD) festival, which serves as a platform for critical debate on local issues with participants from both home and abroad.

Damon Rich is a designer, urban planner, and partner at Hector in Newark, New Jersey. He previously served as planning director and chief urban designer for the City of Newark, New Jersey, and is the founder of the Center for Urban Pedagogy (CUP), an internationally recognised nonprofit organisation that uses art and design to increase meaningful civic engagement. His work has been recognised by the MacArthur Fellowship, the American Planning Association National Planning Award, the Cooper Hewitt National Design Award, the Loeb Fellowship in Advanced Environmental Studies at the Harvard University Graduate School of Design (GSD), the MacDowell Colony, and the United States Pavilion at the 11th Venice Architecture Biennale.

Ignacio Saavedra Valenzuela is a Chilean architect. He received his Bachelor of Science and Humanities degree from the Universidad Católica de Chile, and is an associate lecturer at the Universidad de las Américas in Santiago de Chile and Viña del Mar, Chile. He is co-founder and partner at TOMA Architects, a professional collective that operates in Santiago de Chile. The office develops territorial actions and research to generate alternative social ecosystems, the production of which is self-managed, hands-on and constructed with scarce resources.

Leon van Schaik is Emeritus Professor at the School of Architecture and Urban Design, RMIT University, Melbourne. He has written books on spatial thinking, the poetics of architecture and the processes involved in procuring innovative architecture. The practice-based research PhD programme he initiated has become a template for institutions worldwide. His support of local architectural cultures and his leadership in the procurement of exemplary architecture has resulted in some of Melbourne's most distinguished contemporary buildings. He is a founding member of the Academic Court of the London School of Architecture.

Jae Shin is a designer and partner at Hector. She recently served as an Enterprise Rose Architectural Fellow at the New York City Housing Authority (NYCHA), where she facilitated efforts to define and implement design principles for preserving and rehabilitating the city's public housing. She holds degrees in painting from Rhode Island School of Design in Providence, and architecture from Princeton University in New Jersey. Her projects have received support from the MacDowell Colony and the National Endowment for the Arts, and she has led design studios at New Jersey Institute of Technology and Harvard GSD.

Carl Turner is the founding director of Carl Turner Architects and a self-confessed 'maker at heart'. His love of craft permeates his architectural design and often leads to innovative new uses for materials and processes. He lectures widely in the UK and overseas, and is regularly invited to judge awards. He is a member of the Southwark Design Review Panel and a fellow of the RSA. He was elected as National and London Council Member for the RIBA in 2014. He graduated from the Royal College of Art and was an inaugural Research Associate of the Helen Hamlyn Research Centre. In 2017 he was named one of London's most influential people in the *Evening Standard*'s Progress 1000.

Lys Villalba Rubio is a Madrid-based Spanish architect and independent researcher, and co-founder of Zoohaus Collective. She graduated from ETSAM in Madrid, is a visiting scholar at the Columbia University Graduate School of Architecture, Planning and Preservation (GSAPP) in New York and the Tokyo Wonder Site, and a visiting professor at the Lebanese American University New York and Istituto Europeo di Design (IED), Madrid. Her work explores the intersection of architecture and social, technological and political realms. She previously worked at Foreign Office Architects (FOA), Herzog & de Meuron, Izaskun Chinchilla Architects and *Arquitectura Viva* magazine.

Finn Williams is the co-founder and chief executive officer of Public Practice, a social enterprise building a new generation of planners to shape places for the public good. He previously worked for the Office for Metropolitan Architecture (OMA), Croydon Council and the Greater London Authority (GLA). He is a CABE Built Environment Enabler, Centre for London Associate, Visiting Professor of the Institute for Innovation and Public Purpose, and a member of the Raynsford Review Task Force. He also founded the public-sector planning think tank NOVUS, and was co-curator of the British Pavilion at the 2016 Venice Architecture Biennale.

What is Architectural Design?

Founded in 1930, *Architectural Design* (△) is an influential and prestigious publication. It combines the currency and topicality of a newsstand journal with the rigour and production qualities of a book. With an almost unrivalled reputation worldwide, it is consistently at the forefront of cultural thought and design.

Each title of △ is edited by an invited Guest-Editor, who is an international expert in the field. Renowned for being at the leading edge of design and new technologies, △ also covers themes as diverse as architectural history, the environment, interior design, landscape architecture and urban design.

Provocative and pioneering, △ inspires theoretical, creative and technological advances. It questions the outcome of technical innovations as well as the far-reaching social, cultural and environmental challenges that present themselves today.

For further information on △, subscriptions and purchasing single issues see:

http://onlinelibrary.wiley.com/journal/15542769

Volume 87 No 5
ISBN 978 1119 152644

Volume 87 No 6
ISBN 978 1119 340188

Volume 88 No 1
ISBN 978 1119 379515

Volume 88 No 2
ISBN 978 1119 254416

Volume 88 No 3
ISBN 978 1119 332633

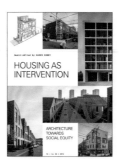

Volume 88 No 4
ISBN 978 1119 337843